Fatal Violence

Case Studies and Analysis
of Emerging Forms

Fatal Violence

Case Studies and Analysis of Emerging Forms

Ronald M. Holmes
Stephen T. Holmes

CRC Press
Taylor & Francis Group
Boca Raton   London   New York

CRC Press is an imprint of the
Taylor & Francis Group, an **informa** business

CRC Press
Taylor & Francis Group
6000 Broken Sound Parkway NW, Suite 300
Boca Raton, FL 33487-2742

© 2010 by Taylor and Francis Group, LLC
CRC Press is an imprint of Taylor & Francis Group, an Informa business

No claim to original U.S. Government works

Printed in the United States of America on acid-free paper
10 9 8 7 6 5 4 3 2 1

International Standard Book Number: 978-1-4398-2687-4 (Hardback)

Library of Congress Cataloging-in-Publication Data

Holmes, Ronald M.
    Fatal violence : case studies and analysis of emerging form / Ronald M. Holmes and Stephen T. Holmes.
        p. cm.
    Includes bibliographical references and index.
    ISBN 978-1-4398-2687-4
    1. Violent crimes--Case studies. 2. Violent deaths--Case studies. 3. Homicide--Case studies. 4. Violence--Case studies. I. Holmes, Stephen T. II. Title.

HV6493.H65 2010
364.15--dc22   2009052532

**Visit the Taylor & Francis Web site at
http://www.taylorandfrancis.com**

**and the CRC Press Web site at
http://www.crcpress.com**

Tootie Holmes,
Ron's wife

Amy Holmes,
Steve's wife

Contents

Preface

As a coroner and academician, we have seen many examples of death motivated by hate. We have also compiled a series of books dealing with serial murder, mass murder, suicide, sex crimes, and other topics of personal violence. We have had the opportunity to interview serial killers in prison, correspond with multiple other serialists, and talk with violent rapists who have wreaked havoc on many unfortunate people. In some fashion, we have become fascinated with the topic of violence.

With the interviews we have learned firsthand as the experts in the field talk about how they planned their crimes. One serialist, presently on death row at San Quentin, was one of the most vocal. He said that he enjoyed most the planning and the execution of the crime rather than the actual murder. One reason for this, he added, was that once the apprehension was accomplished, the victim was no longer a human being but an object. He told a story about how he cut off the heads of many of his victims, placed the heads in the freezer of his refrigerator, and retrieved them when he wanted to have sex. He said this on death row with his girlfriend, whom he later married, sitting next to him.

Another killer said that he lived in a world of fantasy. He constantly thought of killing blond-haired, blue-eyed, unmistakably young, very definitely female, cheerleader types. This was his ideal victim type. He was successful, he said, scores of times. He too gave this information in the visiting room with his girlfriend, whom he would later marry, sitting next to him.

We talked with a young woman who killed her week-old son. She said she loved the child but the devil spoke to her and made her knife the baby to death. Another young woman killed her two daughters, both under age 10. She then committed suicide. She knifed the girls to death and shot herself to death. In her suicide note, she mentioned that the girls were filled with parasites. She "had" to kill them to rid them of the parasites. Her husband had committed suicide 2 years earlier.

We have also talked with street gang members who talk about the injustices in the world and feel no remorse in killing others for turf issues, drug concerns, or horning in on their girlfriends.

Violence is an addictive topic. Even from our perspective, we see violence from a safe perspective. We can look at the violent, talk with the violent, and then go home to our safe refuge in the suburbs where one of the biggest problems is making sure the garage door is shut so no one can come into the garage to steal your lawn mower.

In the course of any book, we have made connections, friends, and, thankfully, no enemies. The contacts we have made in this book helped us with information and ideas. Names come to us and to mention some we run the risk of leaving some out. But that is the risk we will take: David Rivers, retired sergeant of the Cold Case Squad of Miami-Dade Police Department; Thomas Harris, author; Anne Rule, author; and various killers and other violent offenders we have talked with. There are others. We are also especially grateful to the CRC Press. This is our first book with the company. We appreciate its willingness to take a risk with this book.

And of course we thank our families. My (RMH) 6-year-old granddaughter, Bella, was surprised when she found out that Grandpa and Uncle Steve wrote a book. She said, "I thought people had to be really smart to write a book!" Little does she know. Our wives also deserve special thanks.

About the Authors

Dr. Ronald M. Holmes is a professor emeritus at the University of Louisville. He retired at the University of Louisville after 28 years as a professor. He then was elected as coroner in Louisville, the sixteenth largest jurisdiction in the United States. He retired this past year and has returned to the university. He received his doctorate at Indiana University. Dr. Holmes has published books on various subjects including psychological profiling, sex crimes, mass murder, suicide, and other criminal justice topics. He has also published in various journals in *Justice Quarterly, The New England Journal of Civil Confinement, Federal Probation, The Journal Sciences, Men's Health, Police Chief* and many others.

Dr. Holmes's present research interests include the occult (Satanism, Santeria and Palo Mayombe) and motorcycle gangs.

Dr. Stephen T. Holmes is an associate professor of criminal justice and former associate dean of graduate studies and technology at the University of Central Florida. Prior to this position, he served as a social science analyst for the National Institute of Justice in Washington, D.C. He has written more than nine books and eighteen articles dealing with policing, drug testing, probation and parole issues, and violent crime. He also has served a either a principal investigator or consultant on numerous federal, state and local grants and contracts. He received his doctorate from the University of Cincinnati.

Chapter 1

Personal Violence in the United States—Suicide

Introduction

Perhaps nothing affects society more than the loss of human life. This is made more evident in cases of suicide. The intentional taking of one's life is seldom seen necessary. When a young person kills himself or herself over the loss of a relationship or even as seeing life as unbearable because of an incurable disease is seldom judged by the living as being a justified reason.

It is even more difficult to understand when the person committing suicide is young. It is often said that they barely had the opportunity to experience life, they had so much to look forward to, and their whole lives were in front of them, and so on. It is a mystery to many who themselves have lived through pain and suffering; war and prison camp sentences; diseases and illnesses; and deaths of spouses, parents, and others. They lived through it, so how could others not do the same?

But of course we are not all the same. We are truly all different. We all cannot have the same life experiences and react in the same way. Perhaps it is solely our heredity, or maybe it is our total environment. Or more likely it is the unique combination of biology and environment that makes us react in certain fashions to life's circumstances. One thing is true: We are all different.

Suicide in the United States

Suicide is a pervasive problem in today's society. The form may change, and it has over the years. For example, in today's world, suicide bombers, in countries including Iran, Iraq, and Pakistan, are spreading terror and death to innocent people through the use of suicide bombers. This is not only a contemporary behavior. In World War II, the Japanese suicide bombers crashed their planes into the side of American and Allied ships. Even before that, military fighters would go into battle with the expressed intent on offering their lives for a cause before ultimate victory, a religious message, and another altruistic reason.

Regardless suicide is a human behavior that is strictly human. Animals are not known for intentionally offering their lives for others despite whatever anthropomorphic reason is offered. The early church martyrs offered their lives in the hope that by doing so it would in some fashion guarantee their everlasting salvation in the next life. In classic literature, Romeo died in the arms of his lover, Juliet. Because Juliet could not envision living without him, she took her own life. This same message has been offered a multitude of times.

Case Study

In Louisville, Kentucky, a 16-year-old boy was despondent over the imminent possibility that his parents would discover that he was using the Internet to look at porn sites. On his cell phone he had also text messaged his girlfriend more than four thousand times in the last month. That cost, he believed, was also soon to be discovered. Additionally, his girlfriend had just broken up with him and was leaving him for another boy who attended the same high school. Despondent, rejected in his mind, and fearful of punishment concerning his porn viewing and the phone bill soon to arrive, he decided that the only way out was to commit suicide.

He drove to a parking lot in a mall, placed his father's shotgun between his legs, aimed the gun to his face, and pulled the trigger. His suicide note is shown in Figure 1.1.

Many other cases of suicide occur with unexplained logical reasons. In another case, two college professors committed suicide in their apartment. Their pet bird was left with ample food and water for several days. Their note stated, in part, they were tired of living and wanted to spend the rest of eternity in peace, together. They overdosed together, dying in each other's arms. The professors both had tenure. Their salaries together were sufficient for their needs and wants. They were

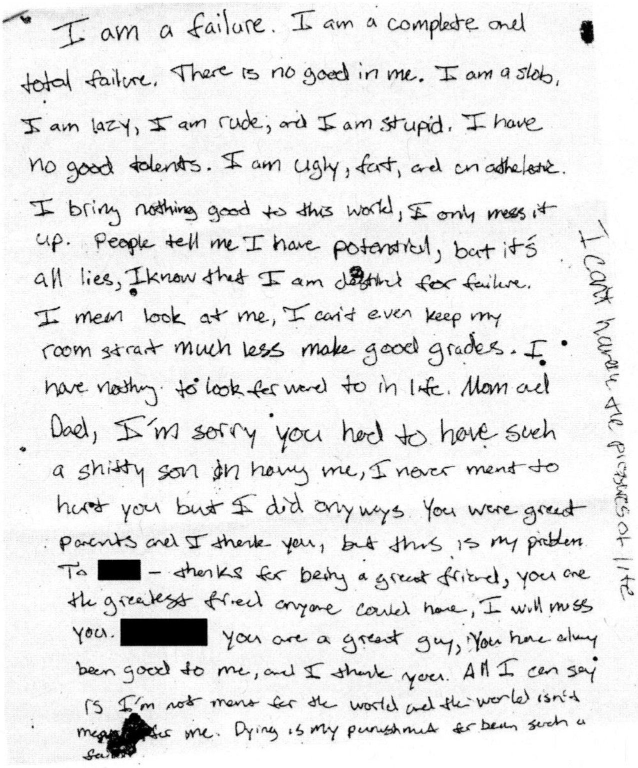

I am a failure. I am a complete and total failure. There is no good in me. I am a slob, I am lazy, I am rude, and I am stupid. I have no good talents. I am ugly, fat, and an athlete. I bring nothing good to this world, I only mess it up. People tell me I have potential, but it's all lies, I know that I am destined for failure. I mean look at me, I can't even keep my room straight much less make good grades. I have nothing to look forward to in life. Mom and Dad, I'm sorry you had to have such a shitty son owning me, I never meant to hurt you but I did anyways. You were great parents and I thank you, but this is my problem. To ▓▓ — thanks for being a great friend, you are the greatest friend anyone could have, I will miss you. ▓▓▓▓ you are a great guy, You have always been good to me, and I thank you. All I can say is I'm not meant for the world and the world isn't meant for me. Dying is my punishment for being such a fai

(margin note: I can't handle the pressures of life)

Figure 1.1   Teenager's suicide note.

respected academics and contributed to their fields of study. They both were in good health, in no financial distress, and very much in love with each other. What possible reason could they have had to die? They knew the reasons, and the reasons were adequate for their determination to end their own lives.

Other cases of suicide are easier to understand. For example, an 89-year-old woman decided to end her life. She neatly arranged her bankbooks, bank statements, insurance papers, and other such important documents on the kitchen table. She called her son and told him of her decision. He lived only a short distance away from his mother, but before he could reach her home, she had already pulled the trigger and shot herself in the forehead. He found all the important documents on the kitchen table as she had left them. He also found on the wall of the kitchen a calendar that she had crossed off the dates until the day she determined would be last day alive.

In yet another case, a 24-year-old lesbian decided to end her life. Her lover had left her after a two-year relationship. Devastated at her loss and with no words to

Figure 1.2   A 76-year-old woman took her life by drug overdose. The reason was expressed in a suicide note she left on a table next to her bed. She was tired of living in pain and alone.

express her feelings, she shot herself. The only note she left was a short sentence she wrote on the living room mirror with her lipstick, "I loved you!"

Suicide in Cohorts

Suicide has been a subject of extensive study in the last decade. Researchers have examined suicide from various perspectives and arrived at different causes, both social and biological. Much of the research has focused on adults who commit suicide. Some do it for health reasons, some for relationship problems, and others for financial reasons (Holmes and Holmes, 2006).

Police

For example, Perin (2007) has painstakingly researched the continuing problem of suicide in the police ranks. She reports, for example, that 97 percent of police officers use their service weapon to take their lives. The data suggests that the officers resort to suicide for a variety of reasons. First, the stress of their jobs contributes significantly to their decisions. There are other reasons including shift work, pending retirement, unsupportive management, and various physical ailments. The total involvement of many officers in their work may result in the officer becoming isolated from other social institutions such as family, friends, and the community. Because of this isolation, depression and a sense of social isolation may result. The manner in which the police officer views the world may hinder any flexibility and heighten the risk factors for suicide. Kelly and Martin (2006) stress that policing agencies must develop strategies and become committed to combating suicide. Educational and intervention programs must be developed. Counseling services, expanding insurance coverage for counseling, and family services must be provided.

Corrections

Suicide in correctional institutions has been an increasing research area despite the rate of suicide has been decreasing in the last twenty-five years (Perry and Olason, 2009). Regardless of the decrease, suicide is still a very real and present danger. Numbers alone do not reflect the human tragedy of suicide. A high rate of suicide in correctional institutions rests with the attitudes of the correctional officers toward the inmates. The issues of fairness, respect, and personal safety are leading items of concern for inmates. When these social items and concerns have risen to the point of extreme importance for the inmate, suicide may be viewed as a functional alternative to incarceration.

There are certain risk factors involved as far as inmates are concerned and the practice of suicide. Certain factors relating to suicide in a correctional facility, include (www.yellowribbon.org/warningsigns/html):

- the view of incarceration as a punishment and disgrace
- denial of membership in decent, law-abiding society
- loss of control over life
- loss of privacy
- loss of family and friends
- concerns over a transfer, appeal, or parole decisions
- the closed social system of the prison (for example, "cons" versus the authorities)
- an atmosphere of violence, fear, and distrust

But what about the personal characteristics of the inmates who commit suicide? These include (Holmes and Holmes, 2006):

- deprived family background typified by abuse and/or criminality
- history of violence
- distress about financial situations
- a history of psychiatric treatment, hospitalization or outpatient
- current physical or mental health problems
- drug and/or alcohol abuse

There may be other traits or characteristics to look at. For example, Kruttschnitt and Vuolo (2007) found that with female inmates youthfulness and a prior history of self-harm—20 percent reported at least one prior suicide attempt according to (Holmes and Holmes, 2006)—play a vital role in the decision to take one's life. The female inmates (Charles et al., 2003) also offer an interesting statement: the feelings of closeness to the correctional staff may increase a woman's risk to suicide and increase suicidal ideation. This certainly needs additional research.

Location and Suicide

The United States has a suicide rate of 12.0 per 100,000 people. In examining the suicide rates of various countries, the United States is ranked 45th among 95 countries. The country with the highest suicide rate is Lithuania with a rate of 38.6. Other countries with high suicide rates include:

■ Russia, 34.3
■ Japan, 24.0
■ Switzerland, 17.4
■ Poland, 15.5
■ China, 13.9
■ Ireland,12.7

Countries with low suicide rates include:

■ Spain, 8.2
■ Italy, 7.1
■ England, 7.0
■ Israel, 7.2
■ Brazil, 4.1
■ Mexico, 3.1

The regions of the United States have differing rates of suicide (Holmes and Holmes, 2006). For example,

■ Northeast, 9.3
■ Midwest, 11.4
■ South, 13.1
■ West, 14.1

There has been some thought that large cities such as New York, Boston, and the cities of business and money lead to self-destruction (Durkheim, 1951). However, the statistics hold that the suicide rates do not necessarily hold that to be true. But we can look at large cities such as Seattle, San Francisco, and Los Angeles in the region of the west, which has a high rate of suicide, as does the southern region with cities such as Atlanta and Miami. It is probably true that there is an abundance of factors involved in the decision to end one's life than simply geographical location.

Occupation and Suicide

Part of the urban legend concerning suicide and occupation has centered on certain occupations as being more conducive to suicide than others. It may be that the stress involved in some occupations is a better indicator of the act of taking one's life than the occupation itself (Foxhall, 2001). For example, Foxhall (2001) found that certain occupational groups are more at risk for suicide than others. He found that the occupations of dentist, artist, machinist, auto mechanic, and carpenter had higher rates of suicide than clerk, elementary school teacher, and cook. He also reported that both male and female physicians had an extremely high rate of suicide

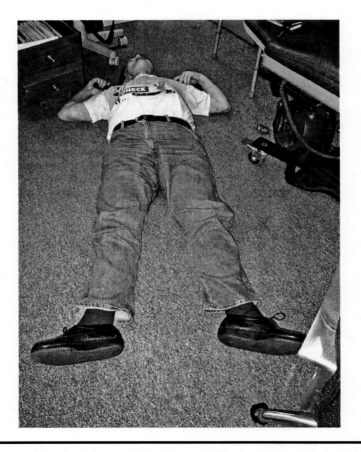

Figure 1.3 **This physician ended his own life because of impending legal charges.**

partly due to the stress they encounter in their work and the easy access they have to means to end their lives, such as drugs and poisons.

Other researchers report from their work that people involved in the military and law enforcement have a high rate of suicide as well as those involved in the mining and farming industries (Kimberlin, 2007).

It may simply be that the various researchers report different groups having differing rates of suicide, and the true picture may be that the occupation itself has little if anything to do with suicide (Holmes and Holmes, 2006). The true picture of the decision to commit suicide stems from the stresses arising from various life circumstances and stressors, and the means to combat those stressors (Foxhall, 2001).

Violent Crimes in the United States

Violence is prevalent and increasing. What are crimes of violence? Violent crimes are defined as:

- Murder and nonnegligent manslaughter—The willful (nonnegligent) killing of one human being by another. Deaths caused by negligence, attempts to kill, assaults to kill, suicides, and accidental deaths are excluded. Justifiable homicides are classified separately (Bureau of Justice, 2003).
- Forcible rape—The carnal knowledge of a female forcibly and against her will. Rapes by force and attempts or assaults to rape regardless of the age of the victim are included. Statutory offenses (no force used, victim under age of consent) are excluded.
- Robbery—The taking or attempting to take anything of value from the care, custody, or control of a person or persons by force or threat of force or violence, and/or by putting the victim in fear (Bureau of Justice, 2003).
- Aggravated assault—An unlawful attack by one person upon another for the purpose of inflicting severe or aggravated bodily injury. This type of assault usually is accompanied by the use of a weapon or by means likely to produce death or great bodily harm. Simple assaults are excluded (Bureau of Justice, 2003).

Property Crime

Property crime includes the following offenses (Bureau of Justice Statistics, 2003):

- Burglary (breaking or entering)—The unlawful entry of a structure to commit a felony or a theft. Attempted forcible entry is included.

- 'Larceny-theft (except motor vehicle theft)—The unlawful taking, carrying, leading, or riding away of property from the possession or constructive possession of another. Examples are thefts of bicycles or automobile accessories, shoplifting, pocket-picking, or the stealing of any property or article that is not taken by force and violence or by fraud. Attempted larcenies are included. Embezzlement, confidence games, forgery, worthless checks, and so forth are excluded.
- Motor vehicle theft—The theft or attempted theft of a motor vehicle. A motor vehicle is self-propelled and runs on the surface and not on rails. Motorboats, construction equipment, airplanes, and farming equipment are specifically excluded from this category.
- Arson—Any willful or malicious burning or attempt to burn, with or without intent to defraud, a dwelling house, public building, motor vehicle or aircraft, personal property of another, etc.

Homicide Rates in the United States

The homicide rate in the United States has changed little since 2000 (Figure 1.4). In 2001 the rate was 7.1 per 100,000. In 2004, the latest statistics available, the rate was 5.9. In the 1970s to 2005, the homicide rate averaged .01. The homicide rate in 2001 included the 9/11 terrorist attack (FBI Uniform Crime Report [UCR], 2009). But in general, homicide victimization rates are higher for very young children than older children who have the lowest rates of all age groups; older teens and young adults have the highest rates of victimization (Bureau of Justice Statistics, 2009). After age 25, victimization rates decline with age.

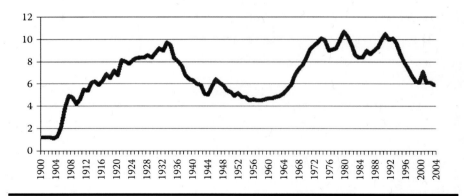

Figure 1.4 Homicide rate, 1900–2004, rate per 100,000 population. (FBI Uniform Crime Report, 2009.)

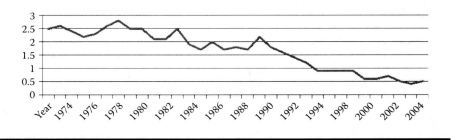

Figure 1.5   Rape rates adjusted victimization rate per 1,000 persons age 12 and over. (FBI Uniform Crime Report, 2009.)

Rape

Because there are some rapes that are not reported, the exact number is unknown. The data provided by the FBI in Figure 1.5 is for rape victims above the age of 12. But what is said about the victims under 12 is that is most cases the rape is performed on the child by someone the child knows, oftentimes a relative.

Assault

Assault is broken into the following categories:

- Aggravated assault—Attack or attempted attack with a weapon, regardless of whether or not an injury occurred, and attack without a weapon when serious injury results.
- Injury—An attack without a weapon when serious injury results or an attack with a weapon involving any injury. Serious injury includes broken bones, lost teeth, internal injuries, loss of consciousness, and any unspecified injury requiring two or more days of hospitalization.
- Simple assault—Attack without a weapon resulting either in no injury, minor injury (for example, bruises, black eyes, cuts, scratches, or swelling) or in undetermined injury requiring less than two days of hospitalization. Also includes attempted assault without a weapon.

In examining the data, it is apparent that the number of aggravated assaults and simple assaults has dropped since 1980 (FBI UCR, 2009). From 1980 to 2000, the rate of aggravated assaults was 10.1 per 100,000. For simple assault, the rate was 27.47. For aggravated assaults from 2000 to 2005 the rate was 4.75, and for simple assaults the rate was 15.25 (Figure 1.6).

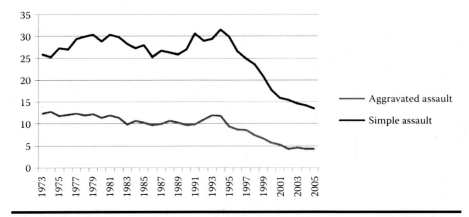

Figure 1.6 Assault rates adjusted victimization rate per 1,000 persons age 12 and over. (FBI Uniform Crime Report, 2009.)

Effects of Exposure to Violence

There probably exist few if any people who were not exposed to some form of violence in their youth. Since it was not simply one act of violence but a combination of events that were violent in their nature, it is very difficult to state that exposure to some type of violence will leave an imprint upon the child and cause the child to become violent. This is especially true when a child has been exposed to continuing acts of violence throughout his early childhood (Zeenah and Scheeringa, 1997). It is not unusual for children exposed to violence to show various signs of stress in their behavior: trouble with school work; having trouble making and keeping friends; smoking; using drugs; or having stomachaches, headaches, or other physical ailments, including posttraumatic stress disorder (Jenkins and Bell, 1997; Osofsky, 1999). It may also be that a child's exposure to violence results in feelings of insecurity and competence in their environment (Marans and Adelman, 1997). Perry (1997) reports that brain development may also be affected by exposure to violence, which Jenkins and Bell (1997) state may also have an effect on the development of the child's personality and belief system as well as their sense of morality.

Witnessing violence is learning violence (Schaffner, 2007). It has no social redeeming values and only causes pain, suffering, arrested development, and hurt in others. But we are a society of violence. We see that in many ways and many examples in the media. In many TV representations, we are taught that violence is a good thing. We reward the characters played by such actors as Steven Seagal, Sylvester Stallone, and others who punch, slice, and kill their way to get what they want, as winning their just war. Witnessing violence is learning violence including the many effects it carries with it.

Conclusion

There are many forms of violence, including suicide, that are extant in this culture at this time. Statistics indicate that perhaps some acts of violence are on the downswing, but any acts of violence must be seen as a significant social problem and something must be done on every level of our society to combat the acts and the subsequent consequences. This should be our goal regardless of the type of violence. In other times violence was permitted and in some cases encouraged. In the not too distant past, acts of violence were encouraged and violence was not unlawful against children and people of subordinate groups, for example, Irish immigrants and Jewish people. Now in the United States, there is a rise in violent acts committed against Hispanics. Who will be the next group?

But for now, let us study the various types of violence currently being used against the out-groups in our society. The forthcoming chapters were selected for discussion after talking to our classes at the Universities of Louisville and Central Florida. We have included them in the order of their preferences. It is an interesting order, and some will find it strange what is included and excluded. But regardless of the preferences others may have, it is a reflection of what the ruling class of the future thinks are the most important topics.

Discussion Questions

1. What prevents you from being more violent? Discuss with your group.
2. One way I try to be nonviolent is _____. Discuss with your group.
3. The most common form of violence I commit is _____.
4. The statement, "Children reflect what they see," perhaps has important implications for children witnessing violence. Discuss with your group.
5. Have you ever been a victim of personal violence? How and what was your reaction?

References

Charles, A., Grilo, C., Fehon, D., Axelrod, S., and McGlashan, T. (2003). Correlates of suicide risk in juvenile detainees and adolescent inpatients. *Journal of American Academy of Child and Adolescent Psychiatry* 42(2): 235–240.

Durkheim, E. (1951). *Suicide: A study in sociology.* (J.A. Spaulding & G. Simpson, trans.) New York: Free Press.

Foxhall, K. (2001). Suicide by profession. *Monitor on Psychology* 32(1): 1–3.

Holmes, R., and Holmes, S. (2006). *Suicide.* Thousand Oaks, CA: Sage.

Jamison, K. (1999). *Night falls fast: Understanding suicide.* New York: Knopf.

Jenkins, E., and Bell, C. (1997). Exposure and response to community violence among children and adolescents. In *Children in a violent society,* ed. by J. D. Osofsky, 9–31. New York: Guilford Press.

Kelly, P., and Martin, R. (2006). Police suicide is real. *Law and Order* 54(3): 93–95.

Kimberlin, J. (2007). Out of the darkness: The secret tragedy of suicide. *The Virginian-Pilot* (http://hamptonroads.com/node/67631, accessed February 15, 2010), July 8.

Kruttschnitt, C., and Vuolo, M. (2007). Cultural context of women prisoners' mental health: A comparison of two prison systems. *Punishment and Society* 9(2): 115–150.

Marans, S., and Adelman, A. (1997). Experiencing violence in a developmental context. In *Children in a violent society*, ed. J. D. Osofsky, 202–222. New York: Guildford Press.

Osofsky, J. (1999). The impact of violence on children. *The Future of Children* 9(3): 33–49.

Perin, M. (2007). Police suicide. *Law Enforcement Technology* 34(9): 8–16.

Perry, A., and Olason, D. (2009). A new psychometric instrument assessing vulnerability to risk of suicide and self-harm behavior in offenders: Suicide concerns for offenders in prison environment (SCOPE). *International Journal of Offenders* 53(4): 385–400.

Perry, B. (1997). Incubated in terror: Neurodevelopmental factors in the "cycle of violence." In *Children in a violent society*, ed. J. D. Osofsky, 124–149. New York: Guilford Press.

www.yellowribbon.org/warningsigns/html

Zeanah, C., and Scheeringa, M. (1997). The experience and effects of violence in infancy. In *Children in a violent society*, ed. J. D. Osofsky, 97–123. New York: Guildford Press.

Suggested Reading

Associated Press. (2001). McVeigh offers little remorse in letters. *The Topeka Capital Journal*, June 10 (accessed June 6, 2009).

Bard-Windie, P., and Badeer, E. (2001). *Targets of hatred: Anti-abortion terrorism*. New York: St. Martin's Press.

Barry, S., and Gualdem, N. (2006). The greatest epidemics in history. *L'Historie*, June, 47.

CNN News. (2006, January 20.). Transcripts.

Ehrman, B. (2003). *Lost scriptures: Books that did not make it into the Bible*. New York: Oxford University Press.

Flannery, E. (1985). *The anguish of the Jews: Twenty-three centuries of anti-Semitism*. New York: Paulist Press.

Goitein, S. (1988). *A Mediterranean society: The Jewish communities of the Arab world as portrayed in the documents of the Cairo Geniza*. Los Angeles: University of California Press.

Gross, D. (2005). Eric Rudolph lays out the argument that fueled his two-year bomb attacks. *San Diego Union-Tribune*, 1.

Hamm, M. (2003). *In bad company: American terrorist underground*. Boston: Northeastern Press.

Hegeman, R. (2009). Suspected killer warns of more violence. *The Courier Journal*, June 8, A-1.

Hewitt, C. (2003). *Understanding terrorism in America: From Klan to Al Qaeda*. New York: Routledge.

Michel, L., and Herneck, D. (2001). *American terrorists: Timothy McVeigh and the Oklahoma City bombing*. New York: Regan Books.

Mlakar, P., Corley, W., Sozen, M., and Thornton, C. (2000). Blast loading and response of Murrah Building. *Forensic Engineering*, 36–43.

Morrison, B. (2006). Special report: Eric Rudolph writes home. *USA Today*, July 6.

NARAL Pro-Choice America Foundation. (2006). Clinic violence and intimidation. *Colorado Springs Gazette*, September 21.

Norman, B. (2003). Hill lives in world of black and white. *Pensacola News Journal*, August 4, 1.

Rappord, R. (2005). Olympic bomber Rudolph calls Supermax home. *Colorado Springs Gazette*, September 14.

Roe v. Wade, 410 U.S. 113 (1973).

Slepian, B. (2006). My father's abortion war. *The New York Times*, January 22.

Chapter 2

Street Gangs

Introduction

Youth street gangs started in New York, Chicago, and Los Angeles in the early 1960s. Many of the gangs started as a means of self-protection and social action, providing activities and a sense of belonging and identity to the young people in the neighborhoods. However as time passed, the gangs became involved in crimes including murder, drug trafficking, and other criminal activities. The activities of the gang of the 1960s and 1970s were much different from the East End Kids of Leo Gorcey and Huntz Hall. Gangs such as the Crips, the Bloods, the 18th Street Gang, and the Latin Kings soon gave the public a new image of what street gangs were all about. Some of the most notorious and dangerous criminals in the United States are part of one gang. It's not the Bloods, it's not the Crips, but a gang called MS-13 (Cosby, 2006).

GANG SLANG

Green light—Order to kill.

GANG STRUCTURE

1. O.G.—Original gangster. They are in it forever.
2. Hardcore—Comprise approximately 5 to 10 percent of the gang. These are the die-hard gangsters, who thrive on the gang's lifestyle

and will always seek the gang's companionship. The hardcore gangsters will most always be the leaders and without them the gang may fall apart. The gang's level of violence will normally be determined by the most violent hardcore members. They are usually the shooters.

3. Regular members (or associates)—Usually range in age from 14 to 17 years old; their jobs are robbing and stealing. They are money oriented. They are initiated into the gang and will back up the hardcore gang members. If they stay in the gang long enough, they will become hardcore. They usually join the gang for status and recognition. They will wear gang colors, attend gang functions, and may even participate in some gang-related criminal activity to fulfill their emotional need of belonging.

4. Wannabes—Usually 11 to 13 years old; their jobs are tagging and stealing. They are not yet initiated into the gang, but hang around with them and usually will do most anything the gang members ask of them so that they may prove themselves worthy of belonging.

5. Could-bes—Usually under the age of 10. Children of this age are at more risk when they live in or close to an area where there are gangs or have a family member who is involved with gangs. It is important to find alternatives for these children so that they may avoid gang affiliation completely. Generally, the further into a gang that someone is, the harder it is to get out.

Source: www.geocities.com/Athens/4111/nogangs.html

The gangs became more visible wearing certain colors (for example, the Crips blue and the Bloods red) and wear certain articles of clothing with self-made emblems or of certain sports clubs (Friedman, 2009). Also, many clubs were started based on the ideas of the aforementioned gangs and became gangs loosely affiliated with the more powerful gangs. But what we will be discussing in this chapter are the well-known street gangs. One book could not contain all the gangs that exist. But if one speaks of the Crips, Bloods, MS-13, and the Latin Kings, one can get an idea of what a street gang is and the nuances of membership and behavior.

Also we must bear in mind that there are different gangs within the "major" gang. For example, there are "sets" as they are called, smaller gangs who call themselves Bloods, and believe they are a part of the larger and more well-known gang.

So, let us start with street gangs, the various ones, and the traits and characteristics of those selected.

The Crips

The Crips are one of the largest youth gangs in the United States. The gang was founded in 1971 in Los Angeles. There is some debate regarding the founding member of the Crips: some experts in the field say that Stanley "Tookie" Williams and Raymond Washington met on a street corner in South Central LA and decided to form a gang for protection, brotherhood, and neighborhood pride, and as an agent against the effects of neighborhood violence. Others believe that neither Williams nor Washington were founding members.

GANG SLANG
Back door parole—To die in prison.

The Crips were not the first black gang in LA. Black gangs appear to have been formed in the 1920s with the influx of a large black population at that time. As white flight moved away from South Central Los Angeles, blacks migrated into the areas of Watts, Slauson, and Firestone/Manchester. These areas are now about 90 percent black.

By the 1940s, the black gangs were involved in protection rackets, prostitution, forgery, gambling, and robbery. In the 1950s, although their criminal activities remained the same, the character of the gangs changed. They became "car gangs." They were loosely organized but violent against outside gangs. Fights would break out between rival gangs. But the fights were physical, but seldom involved any deaths. (But that would change as time passed. Whereas gang members of the 1950s would use chains, baseball bats, and other such implements, today's gangs use AK-47s, hand guns, and other lethal weapons.)

In the 1960s, the street gangs moved from crime gangs to political action gangs. Many black groups became involved in activities that promoted the back race. The Black Panthers, a set of the Crips, for example, become a moving force of violence in Los Angeles. Another gang was called the Renegade Slauson Gang (D. Rivers, interview, July 2009), which at one time was thought to be one of the largest gangs in California. It too was joined by youth who wanted to get rich, belong to a social and criminal outlet, and other reasons. The street gang Crips was started in Freemont High School in Los Angeles. Other Crips gangs were started: the East Side Crips, the Westside Crips, the Main Street Crips, the Kitchen Street Gangs, the 5 Deuce Crips, and the Rolling 20 Crips. The color of the Crips is blue. Bandanas, key chains, hats, and other forms of clothing are green. This makes it easier to recognize a gang member, to recognize one's gang, and also makes the gang member recognizable to law enforcement.

By the 1980s, there were 30,000 Crips members in Los Angeles and nearby areas. The majority of these gang members were involved in drugs, especially crack

GANG SLANG

Base head—Cocaine addict.

Roll—MDMA, ecstasy pill.

cocaine. They lived in areas with high rates of unemployment. Because of the social conditions of the time, membership was climbing and the easy money lifestyle of gang members was attractive. The gang members armed themselves with expensive, high quality weapons of protection and predation. They were also able to afford excellent attorneys to help them defeat the justice system.

What happened to the founders of the Crips? Stanley Williams was executed at San Quentin State Prison in 2005. He was convicted of four counts of murder. Raymond Washington was killed in 1979 in a rival gang shooting.

The Bloods

Early in the 1970s, the Crips were becoming more powerful. The units were banding together to wreak havoc on other non-Crips gangs, and several of these gangs, such as the Piru Street Boys, the Bishops, and the Leuder Park Hustlers joined together in an attempt to protect themselves against the Crips. The United Blood Nation, simply called the Bloods, now became a force to deal with as far as the Crips were concerned. Since the Crips were known to associate themselves with the color of blue, the Bloods adopted the color of red. Also, since many were involved in a life of crime, it was soon that the Bloods, as well as the Crips, moved into the prison system in California.

GANG SLANG

Jockers—Incarcerated sexual predators who prey upon weaker inmates, called "punks."

By the turn of the century, the Bloods had become a very violent entity, much more violent than the Crips. Slashings, for example, became an initiation rite for newbies in the gangs. By the early 2001, the Bloods had moved to the East Coast and became active in New York City and New York state. However, Bloods are more loosely organized than the Crips. They will commit their violent acts against other Blood gangs as well as members of other gangs. Bloods are especially violent. They rely upon violence to obtain what they want, for example, money, clothing, and other items of conspicuous consumption. The Bloods draw their membership typically from young males in the schools in impoverished neighborhoods. The membership in the gang will provide the youths with a sense of friendship and belonging as well as obtaining materials gains. Once in a "set," leadership is earned, not voted upon by the gang membership.

GANG SLANG
Half a yard—Fifty dollars.

Outward Signs of the Bloods

How does one recognize a Blood? Like other gangs, the Bloods have a color, red. It also has a symbol of a five-pointed star and a five-pointed crown. The Bloods also have their favorite sports clothing that identifies their favorite teams: the Dallas Cowboys, San Francisco Forty-Niners, the Philadelphia Phillies, and the Chicago Bulls.

GANG SLANG
Slinging rock—Selling crack cocaine.

As far as tattoos are concerned the Bloods from the East Coast are likely to have the dog paw on the right shoulder. Much of the graffiti include the name of the Blood gang or the Blood set. The graffiti often includes the words "Piru Street," the location of the first Blood gang.

THE BLOOD'S ALLIANCES AND RIVALS
The Bloods have their rivals, but they also have their alliances which include: Black Peace Stones; Cobra Stones, Insane Popes, Gaylords, Future Stones, Spanish Lords, Latin Kings, Latin Saints, and Latin Counts. The rivals include: the Crips, Gangster Disciples, the Black Disciples, and the Black Gangsters.

The Bloods also use hand signals. One such hand gesture includes arranging the fingers to spell out the word "blood."

MS-13

Mara Salvatrucha—also known as MS, Mara, or MS-13—is one of the most violent of the youth street gangs in the United States. It is also a criminal gang composed of such ethnic groups as Salvadorans, Hondurans, Guatemalans, and Nicaraguans.

MS-13 CRIMES

On June 22, 2008, a 21-year-old MS-13 gang member shot and killed a father and his two sons after their car briefly blocked the gang member from completing a left turn (*Newsday*, 2008).

In June 2009, Edwin Ortiz, Jose Gomez Amaya, and Alexander Aguilar were MS-13 gang members from Long Island who had mistaken bystanders for rival gang members. As a result, two innocent civilians were shot. Edgar Villalobos, a laborer from El Salvador, was among the dead (Strickler, 2009).

MS-13 was founded in the 1960s. By 1980, to protect Salvadoran immigrants from other gangs in the Los Angeles area, MS-13 moved to Los Angeles. Originally only Salvadorans were allowed to join the gang. This rule was later relaxed and other Central Americans were permitted join. It only took a short time for the gang members to start preying upon other Salvadorians (Gifford, 2007).

Because of the violence and the crimes committed by the MS-13 gang members, once arrested, many were deported back to their home countries. Because of this, many gang members recruited new members from their own countries to reinforce their numbers. In the meantime, the numbers have risen along with their commission of violent crimes. The gang itself has sets across the United States and other countries. There are an estimated 100,000 MS-13 members in 42 states. The gang has been verified in the following cities and states: Atlanta, Chicago, Des Moines, New York City, Washington, D.C., New York state, North Carolina, Virginia, and Edmonton and Vancouver in Canada. It is estimated that there are about 25,000 gang members in El Salvador. But one thing which holds down it membership and, hopefully, violent activities is the lack of a central hierarchy of command (Federal Bureau of Investigation, 2008).

Their penchant for violence makes them the most feared gang in the U.S. Their crimes are typically crimes of violence and include murder, rape, and other forms of personal violence including drug distribution, prostitution, robbery, home invasions, immigration offenses, kidnapping, carjackings/auto thefts, and vandalism. They are also involved in smuggling drugs and importation of illegal aliens. The soldiers in the gangs often have experience in foreign weaponry including the machete. Many times the police have found dismembered and mutilated bodies including some that have been decapitated.

Identifiers

MS-13 gang members have many tattoos on their face and bodies. Their colors are blue and white (Cosby, 2006), the colors of the Salvadoran flag. The ages of the members range from 8 years old to 40 years old. Thirteens are often painted on walls of businesses and sidewalks. It is also a favorite tattoo on the bodies of the gang members (Figure 2.1).

Members of Mara Salvatrucha, like members of most modern American gangs, utilize a system of hand signs for purposes of identification and communication. One of the most commonly displayed is the "devil's head" formed by extending the index and little fingers of the hand while tucking in the middle and ring fingers with the thumb), which forms an M when displayed upside down (Figure 2.1). This hand sign is similar to the symbol commonly displayed by heavy metal musicians and their fans ("Gang uses deportation," 2008).

GANG SLANG

Sweet kid—An inmate who allies with an older, more experienced inmate, for protection or knowledge.

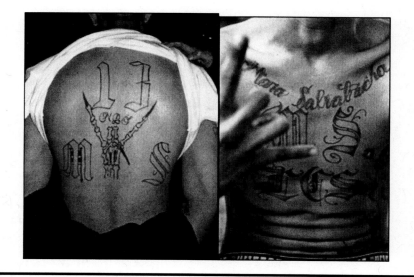

Figure 2.1   Example of gang tattoos and a display of the devil's head.

Employment

Only a few members of the MS-13 are employed and usually in menial employment by presenting false documents showing that they are legal immigrants. Common examples of places where these gang members are employed are jobs in construction, restaurants, delivery services, and landscaping. The reason? Many of these types of employers do not bother to scrutinize personnel records (FBI, 2008).

Initiation and Organization

Young, MS-13 prospective gang members are usually initiated by a "jumping in" ceremony. The prospect will step inside a circle surrounded by gang members. The strongest gang members, usually five of them, will join the inductee in the circle. They will attack, beat, stomp the new member for a count of 13. If the prospect can survive the beating, he is welcomed into the gang.

The soldiers in the gang have a high rate of convictions, if for no other reason, once a MS-13, always a MS-13. If a gang member commits a crime and is taken to court and is found not guilty then he still is a member of MS-13. The leader of the set has to approve the member leaving the gang. Since there is no organized hierarchy of national leadership, when members migrated eastward, they began forming cliques that for the most part operated independently. These cliques, though, often maintain regular contact with members in other regions to coordinate recruitment and criminal activities and to prevent conflicts (FBI, 2008).

We believe MS-13 will continue to be a gang to be reckoned with. With their dedication to violence and with their locations in various parts of the United States, as well as several foreign countries, there does not appear to be any inroads into the work of this very violent gang.

MS-13 LEADER DRAGGED TO COURT TO FACE MURDER CHARGE: TRIES TO FIRE LAWYER, PLEAD GUILTY

First, the reputed head of a violent street gang had to be handcuffed and hauled into a Brooklyn courtroom in a wheelchair after refusing to show up to face charges that he killed a man.

Then, Oscar "Taz" Fuentes, 28, resorted to a bizarre legal strategy in the case that could potentially land him the death penalty—demanding that he be allowed to fire his lawyer and plead guilty.

Fuentes, 28, the accused leader of the MS-13 gang in New York State, was hit with the new murder charge yesterday for allegedly staging the drive-by shooting of an innocent 21-year-old Queens man, Maurice Parker, on May 18, 2007.

"I make my choice your honor," a disheveled Fuentes cried out, as his lawyer asked Brooklyn Federal Judge Sandra Townes to order a mental health evaluation. "If I make something wrong, if I make something illegal, I want to pay for it."

Fuentes, who has been held behind bars for gun possession since 2007, then complained, "When did the case change? I was willing to cooperate and all of a sudden today they don't need my help?"

Assistant U.S. Attorney Jason Jones told the Judge Fuentes was "in a wheelchair, not for health reasons, but because he's a violent gang member who refused to come to court."

Townes entered a not guilty plea for Fuentes and agreed to keep Hurwitz, the attorney, on the case and appoint a second lawyer to represent the accused gang leader while the feds determine whether to seek the death penalty.

"My warning and advice to you is you don't know where to begin with defending yourself," Townes told Fuentes, as the victim's mother looked on from the spectator seats.

The night of the murder, Fuentes and MS-13 soldier Julio Chavez, 23, were driving the streets of Flushing and "looking to commit a drive-by shooting" when they spotted Parker outside a store, Jones wrote in a letter.

Chavez and another gang member allegedly sprung from the car and shot Parker six times, including three shots to the head.

MS-13 is a violent international street gang of immigrants from El Salvador, Honduras, and Guatemala.

Source: **Cornell, K.** *New York Post,* **March 19, 2009, 1.**

The Latin Kings

The Latin Kings are said to be the largest and most organized Hispanic street gang in the United States of America that has its roots dating back to the 1940s in Chicago (Brotherton, 2004). Latin King documents reveal that Gino Gustavo Colon (a.k.a. Lord Gino) is considered the "SUN" of the Almighty Latin King Nation in Chicago—and has been for a long time. Currently he is serving a life sentence in federal prison due to a 25-count indictment, which includes charges of conspiracy to distribute cocaine and other drugs. At the time of this writing, the Latin King headquarters was located on Beach and Spaulding streets in Northwest Chicago.

Originally the gang members were Puerto Ricans, but recently the Latin Kings started admitting members of all races to join. It is now mostly composed of Spanish, Caribbean, Latvian, Italian, Portuguese, Mexicans, and South Americans.

Estimates suggest they have over 25,000 Latin King members residing within Chicago city limits. However, the gang membership is not limited to Chicago. It has organized chapters in various states. These gang sets, or chapters, each report to a leader. The head of the entire criminal organization is known as the Inca.

The Latin Kings think of themselves to be a community-based organization. They preach Hispanic pride; some King chapters have even formed their own religion called Kingdism, with its own prayers, rites, rituals. Meetings are often used by members to discuss plans of action for social events as well as retaliating against other gangs and punishment for breaking gang rules (R. Sanders, interview, 2009).

When compared to most street gangs, the Latin Kings are generally more structured and organized. The gang's rules are strictly enforced and some members celebrate January 6 as King's Holy Day and the first week in March as King's Week.

LATIN KING LEADER SENTENCED IN NJ

TRENTON, N.J.—A leader of the Latin Kings in New Jersey is going to prison for silencing a queen in the street gang.

A judge sentenced Jose "Boom Bat" Negrete to life plus 20 years behind bars for ordering the murder of Jeri-Lynn Dotson and the attempted murder of her roommate, Alex "Alkey" Ruiz in Trenton.

Prosecutors say Dotson was gunned down in 2004 to silence the 23-year-old because she had witnessed Ruiz's abduction.

Before he was sentenced Tuesday, Negrete told the judge the victims were gang members who "chose that lifestyle."

The judge called Negrete a coward who had "others to do your dirty work."

The 26-year-old will be eligible for parole after he serves nearly 81 years in prison.

Source: **Bucci, 2009.**

Other Major Gangs

There are many other gangs in the U.S. In addition to the Latin Kings, another gang from the West Side of Chicago is the Four Corner Hustlers. Formed in 1970, the gang has emerged as a violent force in local gang folklore. The Four Corner Hustlers has been a target for local police; the FBI; Drug Enforcement Administration (DEA); Bureau of Alcohol, Tobacco, Firearms and Explosives (ATF); and U.S. Customs (R. Sanders, interview, 2009). In Chicago in 2008, the local police and federal agents suggest that a majority of all homicides that occurred in the city were the result of gang activity. The exact number is unknown, but there were 229 homicides reported to the police in 2008. It appears that 2009 will show little difference.

The Top Six in South Florida started out in a local high school as a social group, but it soon became involved in a street gang, making money in the usual gang manner. However, the Top Six, named after the original six members of the gang, moved into the world of entertainment by recording rap music videos, which are very violent in content and message. The local and federal agencies in Miami and the surrounding areas have been very successful in the eradication of the Top Six gang. Although the Top Six gang itself has almost dropped out of existence, it has been replaced by smaller splinter groups and gangs. This makes it very difficult law enforcement to successfully investigate the criminal elements of the gangs and make arrests.

Conclusion

Gangs have been a part of American culture for many years. The old time Western gangs, Irish gangs, and Italian mobs and mafia gangs have been replaced by the modern street gangs who now fill the streets with gunshots and violence. There may be as many as 20,000 gangs in the United States with a membership of 100,000. Many gangs are composed of foreign nationals as well as American citizens, who are often disenfranchised youth who join for a variety of reasons including protection, status, and making money. The newer gangs are involved in the illegal drug importation and sales, and even a few are involved in the record and recording industry (e.g., Top Six). Their rap songs are replete with words and music that reflect drugs, killings, and other forms of human violence.

What can be done to lower the risk and the numbers of gangs and gang members? As we have seen with the Top Six gang in Florida, a concentrated effort on the local, state, and federal levels has had some positive effect. A gang eradication plan must be a coordinated effort with a realization that there are multiple reasons for gang members This realization may be the first step. But we must also realize the number of gangs. For example, the following is a list of street gangs in the Chicago area alone:

- Sureno 13
- Almighty Saints
- Black Disciples
- Black P Stones
- Puerto Rican Stones
- Crips
- Bloods
- Vice Lords

- Spanish Lords
- Crazy Hmong Boyz
- True Asian Bloods
- Oriental Thugs
- 12th Street Players
- Four Corner Hustlers
- Gangster Disciples
- Palos Hood
- Mickey Cobras
- Two Six
- Latin Eagles
- Latin Kings
- MS-13
- Maniac Latin Disciples
- Simon City Royals
- TAP Boyz (The Arabian Posse)
- Spanish Gangster Disciples
- Chicago Gaylords
- Latin Kings 13
- Popes (gang)
- Satan Disciples
- Spanish Cobras
- Sureños
- La Raza Nation
- Norteños
- Sons of Silence

In looking at the number of gangs in this list, it is easily seen that Chicago and other large cities like it face a monumental task.

Discussion Questions

1. Discuss the rise in populations of street gangs in Hispanic groups.
2. What popular services do street gangs serve?
3. What are the reasons members join a gang?
4. What do you believe is the role of the media and the glorification of membership in street gangs? How accurate is the portrayal of the street gangs in the media?
5. There is some literature that suggests that there is some movement between street gangs and prison gangs, but there is nothing that suggests the similar movement from street gangs to motorcycle gangs. Why do you believe that would be?

References

Brotherton, D. (2004). *The Almighty Latin King and Queen Nation: Street politics and the transformation of a New York City gang.* New York: Columbia University Press.

Bucci, K. (2009). Latin kings boss found guilty, *Central Jersey and Mercer County News.* Trenton, NJ. May 28 (accessed February 15, 2010).

Cornell, K. (2009). MS-13 leader dragged to court to face murder charge: Tries to fire lawyer, plead guilty. *New York Post*, March 19, 1.

Cosby, R. (2006). MS-13 is one of the nation's most dangerous gangs: In-depth look it members, enemies, and its threat to our national security. *msnbc.com*, February 1, 1.

Federal Bureau of Investigation. (2008). *The MS-13 threat: A national assessment.* www.fbi.gov/page2/jan08/ms13_011408.html (accessed September 5, 2009).

Friedman, L. (2009). *Gangs.* Detroit, MI: Greenhaven Press.

Gang uses deportation to its advantage to flourish in the U.S. (2008). *National Geographic.* (accessed September 10, 2008).

Gifford, C. (2007). *Gangs.* North Manokato, MN: Smart Apple Media.

Strickler, A. (2009). Three Suffolk victims linked by ongoing gang violence. *Newsday.* http://www.newsday.com/long-island/suffolk/three-suffolk-victims-linked-by-ongoing-gang-violence-1.1327241.

Sweeney, A., and Olivo, A. (2009). 4 charged with attempted murder of Chicago cop. *Chicago Tribune*, August 31, A1.

www.geocities.com/Athens/411/nogangs.html

www.newsday.com/long-island (accessed February 15, 2010).

Suggested Reading

Buchanan, P. (2007). *State of emergency: The third world invasion and conquest of America.* New York: St. Martin's Griffin.

Carter, S. A., and Stockstill, M. (2006). Report: MS-13 gang hired to murder Border Patrol. *Daily Bulletin.com*, January 9.

Coolidge, S. (2008). Man, 18, gets life in prison for murder. *Columbus Dispatch.* (accessed November 26, 2008).

Chapter 3

Motorcycle Gangs

Introduction

Since the end of World War II, motorcycle clubs and gangs have been a part of American culture. The names of these gangs are well known to most, names such as the Outlaws, the Sons of Silence, the Mongols, the Hells Angels, the Pagans, and the Bandidos. What started as social groups for many gangs has moved into crime of all types: murder, rape, drugs, smuggling, kidnapping, and other crimes (Richardson, 1991).

What we intend to show in this chapter is the history of an individual gang, its main members, the founder(s), and its goals and viability. While most gang members are law abiding, there are the "one percenters," the 1 percent of the gang population who commit crimes and get in trouble with the authorities (Finlay and Matthews, 1996).

America's Motorcycle Gangs: A Brief History

After WWII, motorcycle gangs became a well-known force on the streets. The motorcycle gangs were social outlets for men returning from the war. As time passed, less emphasis was placed on the social outlets and more on the criminal side of the gang. This is no better illustration than in the groups calling themselves the Hells Angels (Allender, 2001) and the Bandidos (Rijn, Edwards, and Brennan, 2006).

The Bandidos are not the only motorcycle gang that has been involved in trouble with the law. Thirty-seven Sons of Silence members were arrested in 1999 on

Eight men of Toronto, Canada, were found dead in a home at a farm owned by a known member of a local biker gang, the Bandidos. The investigation was not certain if the killings were a result of a gang cleansing or if another motive was involved. One victim was a truck driver who was not a member of the gang but cruised the highways in his tow truck to come to the aid of stranded motorists. The Bandidos have issued a statement denying any involvement in the killings (Rijn, Edwards, and Brennan, 2004).

charges of drug trafficking and illegal weapons in Denver (Nieves, 1999). On Labor Day 2004, two girls, ages 14 and 15, were allegedly taken from their dates near the town of Seaside, California. When the girls were found several hours later, one girl was nude and the other only had on a torn sweater. Soon, four gang members of the Hells Angels were arrested for rape, kidnapping, and other charges (Thompson, 1965). The Hells Angels, based out of California, has been illustrated in movies such as *The Wild One,* starring Marlon Brando, and *Easy Rider.*

In 1995, John Bartolomeo was sentenced to thirty-five years in prison for the murder of a Devils Disciple. He ran over "Cats" Michaels with his car in Massachusetts in retaliation for dealing in drugs in his area, which the Hells Angels consider to be their own turf ("Hells Angel member," 1998).

The crimes of the Outlaws and the Hells Angels are not new. Trethewy and Katz (1998) stated that outlaw motorcycle gangs have had more than 50 years to hone their skills and become a criminal force to be reckoned with. The outlaw motorcycle gangs have outings to solidify their gang unity and also congregate with other gang members to cooperate with criminal elements. Johnson (1981) reported that gang members of these two groups were involved in stealing Harley-Davidson motorcycles and other motor vehicles for almost thirty years in North Carolina.

In 2002 many members of rival motorcycle gangs waged war inside Harrah's Casino in Laughlin, Nevada. The result? Three people were killed and thirteen were taken to a local hospital with gunshot and stab wounds. Witnesses said the two gangs involved in this fatal incident were the Mongols Motorcycle Club and the Hells Angels (Bach, 2002). Mongol Anthony "Bronson" Barrera, 43, was stabbed to death and two Hells Angels, Jeramie Bell, 27, and Robert Tumelty, 50, were shot to death.

In November 2007, Christopher Ablett, 37, an alleged member of the Mongols, was sought in San Francisco on charges that he killed Mark "Papa" Guardado, the head of the Hells Angels Frisco chapter. Police believe Ablett shot Guardado, 46, after what police describe as a "wrestling match" outside a Mission District bar the night of September 2. Witnesses told police that the killer rode away on a motorcycle (Stannard, 2007).

Biker Violence in Other Countries

Biker violence is not restricted to the United States. Germany, for example, has chapters of the Hells Angels and the Bandidos. Deggerich and Stark (2009) report a long-standing history of hostility between the two gangs.

In Canada, in 2006, five bikers were arrested in a case of mass murder in southeastern Ontario. The Royal Canadian Mounted Police report that there are about 1,200 members of motorcycle gangs in Canada. The past president of the Outlaws, Jeffrey LaBrash, was killed in a gunfight with members of other motorcycle gangs (Associated Press, 2006).

In Europe, three motorcycle groups are dominant: the Hells Angels, the Bandidos, and the Outlaws. These gangs are involved in crimes ranging from traditional drug smuggling and vehicle crime to human trafficking and contract killings. They are spreading throughout the European Union but are particularly active in the Nordic countries, Germany, and Belgium. They are also becoming more active in Britain. The main gang activity is drug trafficking. Illegal substances enter the countries through several land and sea routes controlled by different gangs. For example, routes through the Nordic and Baltic region are dominated by Russian-speaking gangs, while the Atlantic area is in the grip of the Dutch, British, and Belgians. These well-established routes have also become corridors for illegal immigration, alcohol, tobacco smuggling, and sex-slave trafficking. Each year, more than 100,000 women and children are trafficked across EU borders. Many end up in forced prostitution in brothels or on the streets of British cities.

In Europe, there are six major biker gangs. The first is the Hells Angels. The British offshoot of the world's most infamous motorcycle gang was born after two English bikers visited the United States and took their impetus from its West Coast birthplace. The group, officially sanctioned in 1969, organizes the Bulldog Bash, one of the biggest biker events in Europe.

The Outlaws had relatively modest beginnings in Illinois in 1935, and by the turn of the century, the Outlaws had grown to encompass 200 chapters around the world. The British arm of the club came under the aegis of its New World forefathers in 2000, and currently boasts followings in Birmingham, London, Kent, and the Forest of Dean. Members flaunt a crossed piston and skull motif on the back of their black leather jackets.

The Blue Angels was founded in Glasgow. Its name derives from Scotland's national colors; some members state the Blue stands for Bastards, Lunatics, Undesirables, and Eccentrics. They began by using stripped-down Triumph/Norton hybrids (without lights) as their ride of choice. Chapters in Leeds and Sheffield first careened onto British roads in 1997.

Road Tramps, formerly known as the Reapers, was established in Ireland in 1987. It is part of the Irish Motorcycle Club Alliance, an umbrella organization drawing together the Vikings, Freewheelers, and Devils Disciples. The Road Tramps also have an English following.

The Bandidos have 2,400 members in 195 chapters, across 14 countries, including groups in Jersey and Guernsey, England (Thompson, 2009).

Devils Disciples can be found in both Ireland and England. The Disciples (originally deliberately misspelled) developed into a criminal gang. The crimes seem to be originally centered on drugs and murder.

Motorcycle Gangs in the United States: The "Big Four"

Gang crimes are often crimes of violence and directed toward other gangs and gang members. The "Big Four" (the Outlaws, the Bandidos, the Pagans, and the Mongols) are continually involved in crimes of violence including murder. While the motorcycle gangs were originally founded around a sense of brotherhood with tavern drinking and social gatherings, it has moved into a terrorist milieu that has enlarged its circle of criminal activity and violence to persons and people outside the gangs (Barker and Human, 2009).

The Outlaws

Perhaps the most noted motorcycle gang in the United States is the Outlaws. Formed by a small group of military veterans after WWII, they were attracted to the Harley-Davidson motorcycle and other choppers. Their goals centered on a sense of brotherhood and a dedication to personal freedom, and nonconformity to overall society's folkways, mores, laws, and institutions. Because of its propensity to crime, the American Motorcycle Association (AMA) does not sanction the group and the Outlaws do not adhere to the rules of the AMA (Drew, 2002).

The command structure of the Outlaws is similar to many other bureaucracies. In many such groups, there is a president, vice president, treasurer, secretary, and sergeant at arms (Jones, 2001). Of course not all Outlaw members are of the criminal bent. There are so-called 'one percenters' who are dedicated criminals. These are members who are the criminals and dedicated to crime and mayhem.

The typical internal organization of a motorcycle club consists of a president, vice president, treasurer, secretary, road captain, and sergeant at arms.

Single, large motorcycle club gangs are called chapters, and the first chapter established for an motorcycle club is referred to as the mother chapter. The president of the mother chapter serves as the president of the entire motorcycle club, and sets club policy on a variety of issues (Jones, 2001).

One percenters—Name given to motorcycle gang members who are considered outlaws. The other 99 percent are considered to be law abiding and social.

ORGANIZATIONAL STRUCTURE OF AN OUTLAW MOTORCYCLE GANG

National president—Often the founder, elected by the gang itself.

Regional Representative—The national vice president.

National enforcer—Bodyguard and answers directly to the president.

Chapter president—Head of a local unit and has authority of all chapter business.

Chapter secretary/treasurer—Collects dues, takes minutes, responsible for finances.

Sergeant at arms—In charge of maintaining order at club meetings.

Road captain—Usually the security chief for sponsored runs or outings.

Source: **Carlie,** *Into the Abyss,* **2002.**

One-percenter motorcycle clubs do not allow women to become full members. Women are submissive to the men, treated as property, victimized by being forced into prostitution or street-level drug trafficking, and are often physically and sexually abused. Any pay women receive is given to their individual men and sometimes to the entire club. Women's roles as well as their status as objects, make these groups completely male dominated and extremely gender segregated (Adler and Adler, 1994; Barker, 2005).

The Patches and Colors of the Outlaws

Not all Outlaws gangs call themselves Outlaws. They may have a different name but still affiliated with the Outlaws in shared membership, ideologies, and goals. Each group has a cloth patch that identifies the wearer of the club one belongs to. Like street gangs mentioned in the previous chapter, motorcycle gangs will wear patches and clothing of different colors. For example, in some groups the wearer may decorate his patch with the color of green. This denotes that the wearer has had sex with a woman with venereal disease. Purple on his patch tells the viewer that he has had sex with a corpse. How true this is and how much it is intended to fool those outside the subculture of the gang is open to debate (Pratt, 2006).

Being fully patched—Being a full member of the motorcycle gang.

The Relationships and Confederation of Outlaws

Periodically, representatives of various motorcycle gang units within a confederation will meet in a neutral area to discuss problems, issues, and disagreements that may exist. The members of the various motorcycle gangs will try to resolve issues without violence and bloodshed. Of course, it stands to reason that the larger and more powerful one-percenter motorcycle gangs usually get their way with the smaller and less powerful gangs. And usually the smaller groups exist at the will of the larger groups.

There are some larger groups at war with other large motorcycle gangs. This holds true, for example, with the gangs such as the Outlaws, the Mongols, and the Hells Angels. Certainly there are times when these large one percenters have fought with one another. In 2002, members of the Mongols and the Hells Angels were involved in a confrontation that left three dead and several wounded. Later in the same year, the Hells Angels and the Pagans (another large one-percenter gang) were involved in a conflict in Long Island in an issue on turf jurisdiction. These are only two examples of the many conflicts that have developed over the years.

Hells Angels

The Hells Angels was founded in the late 1940s in California. Dressed in black with swastikas on their jackets, Hells Angels members garnered international fame as a violent gang when in 1965, it was commissioned to provide security for a Rolling Stones concert. During the course of the concert the Angels went into the crowd and created a violent melee (Thompson, 1996). One concert attendee was killed and several others were injured. In 1970 a battle with another outlaw gang, the Breed, resulted massive injuries, and fifty-seven members of both gangs were charged with murder. Two Breed brothers were castrated and one Angel was killed (Lavigne, 1996; Thompson, 1999).

Sonny Barger expanded the Hells Angels in the 1950s. Barger was jailed in the 1990s for plotting to bomb a rival's clubhouse (Serwer, 1992). Informants inside the gang stated that the members are greatly interested in weapons and have large caches of weapons that rival many small countries (Jeremiah, 2006; Serwer, 1992).

Noted as one of the Big Four of the one percenters, the Hells Angels are involved in various criminal activities including drug trafficking, assault, extortion, murder, prostitution, and trafficking stolen goods. Its memberships include sets across the world, which declare a noncriminal mission of organizing social events, road trips, and efforts to raise money for charitable causes (Lindsey, 2005).

To join the Hells Angels, there is a proscribed requirement. First the candidate must have a driver's license; a working motorcycle; no criminal record as a child molester or pedophile; and cannot have applied for employment as a police officer, correctional officer, or federal law enforcement. After a period of "hanging around" the candidate is awarded a "full patch" after being voted upon by the full membership. The patch must be returned after the member leaves the club (Hall, 2005).

There are an estimated 3,600 full-time members of the Hells Angels across the world (Dobyns, 2009). The membership is likely to grow especially in the United States.

The Bandidos

As with most of the motorcycle gangs were have spoken of, the Bandidos were founded in 1966 in San Leon, Texas. It is a criminal gang, a one percenter. It has a motto: We are the people our parents warned us about (Winterhalder, 2005).

The Bandidos were founded by Don Chambers, a former Marine and veteran of Vietnam. After he was found guilty of murder, the presidency was passed to Ronnie Hodge (Dulaney, 2005). From this beginning forty years ago, the Bandidos have chapters across the world with sets in Europe (Germany and France), Australia, and Southeast Asia (Malaysia and Thailand; Caine, 2009).

This one percenter gang has a long history of criminal activity. In 2006, one member of the Washington set of the Hells Angels. Eighteen members of the motorcycle gang were sentenced to terms in prison for various crimes including conspiracy, witness tampering, and drug and gun violations. In 2004, a man was found fatally stabbed. He was stabbed multiple times. The victim was Robert Quiroga, Super Flyweight Champion of the World. A member of the Bandidos was found guilty of the crime (http://www.woai.com/mostpopular/story.asp?/content-id-d3e0dce-483a-9424-fb66fi3a6260).

The Pagans

The Pagans Motorcycle Club was founded in 1959 in Maryland. The founder was Lou Dobkins, a biochemist at the National Institute of Health. Originally clad in white denim jackets and riding Triumphs, the gang had begun to evolve along the lines of the California stereotype generated by the Outlaws, the Hells Angels, and the Mongols. After its founding, the Pagans quickly turned into a one percent gang, and violence and crime almost became a style of life. Compared to the aforementioned clubs, the Pagans have small numbers. It may have as many as 400 members according to its Internet homepage.

Motto of the Pagans—Respect few, fear none.

Discussion Questions

1. Discussion the differences and similarities of the Big Four Motorcycle Clubs.
2. Discuss the roles of females in the motorcycle gangs.

3. Why do you believe the motorcycle gangs moved from social clubs to gangs of crime?
4. Are there motorcycle gangs in your community? Are they involved with one of the Big Four? Where are they located?
5. Are any motorcycle gangs in your area involved with social and charitable causes? Give examples, if any.

References

Adler, P. A., and Adler, P. (1994). Women in outlaw motorcycle clubs. In *Constructions of deviance: Social power, context, and interaction*, eds. P. A. Adler and P. Adler, 389–401. Belmont, CA: Wadsworth.

Allender, D. (2001). Gangs in middle America. *FBI Law Enforcement Bulletin*, pp. 1–9.

Associated Press. (2006). *8 deaths in Canada linked to biker Gang: Five people arrested on murder charges*. www.nicaso.com/pages/doc_page210.html.

Barker, T. (2005). One percent biker clubs—A description. *Trends in Organized Crime* 9(1): 101–112.

Barker, T., and Human, K. (2009). *Crimes of the Big Four motorcycle gangs*. http://www. ncjrs. gov/app/publications/abstract.aspx?ID=248772.

Bach, L. (2002). Motorcycle gang violence: Laughlin event turns deadly. *Las Vegas Review-Journal*, 1.

Caine, A. (2009). *Befriend and betray: Infiltrating the Hells Angels and other criminal brotherhoods*. New York: MacMillan.

Carlie, M. (2002). *Into the abyss: A personal journey into the world of the street gangs*.

Denson, B. (2008). Police fear violence as outlaw bikers move to Oregon. *Oregon News*, April 20, A-1.

Dobyns, J. (2009). *No angel: My harrowing undercover journey to the inner circle of he Hells Angels*. New York: Crown.

Drew, A. (2002). *The everything motorcycle book: The one book you must have to buy, ride, and maintain your motorcycle*. Avon, MA: Adams Media Corp.

Dulaney, W. (2005). A brief history of outlaw motorcycle clubs. *International Journal of Motorcycle Studies* 1(November).

Finlay, T., and Matthews, C. (1996). *Motorcycle gangs: A literature search*. Toronto: University of Toronto.

Hall, N. (2005). Behind the patch: Angels ABC's. *The Vancouver Sun*, June 10.

Hells Angel member receives 35 year prison sentence. (1998). Motorcycle News Wire. http://www.powersportsnetwork.com/motorcyclenewsdetail/id=1255/newsarticle1255.htm (accessed September 9, 2009).

Jeremiah, D. (2006). *Angels: The strange and mysterious truth*. New York: Multnomah.

Johnson, W. (1981). *Motorcycle gangs and white collar crime*. http://www.ccjrs.gov/app/publications/abstract.aspx?ID=147211.

Jones, B. (2001). *Bike lust*. Madison, WI: University of Wisconsin Press.

Lavigne, Y. (1996). *Hells Angels: Into the abyss*. Toronto: HarperCollins.

Nieves, D. (1999). 37 arrested in raids on Sons of Silence. *The Gazette* (Colorado Springs), Oct. 9. http://findarticles.com/p/articles/mi_qn4191/is_19991009/ai_n9964034/.

Pratt, A. (2006). *Motorcycling, nihilism, and the price of cool: Nihilism and FTW style*. Chicago: Open Court Publishing.

Richardson, A. (1991). *U.S.A. perspective on outlaw motorcycle gangs*. Paper presented to the 17th annual International Motorcycle Gang Conference, Orlando, FL.

Rijn, N., Edwards, P., and Brennan, R. (2006). Biker gangs linked to murders. *The Toronto Star*, April 10, A1.

Serwer, A. (1992). The Hells Angels' devilish business. *Fortune Magazine*, November 30.

Thompson, H. (1965). The motorcycle gangs. *The Nation*, May 17, 1–8.

Thompson, H. S. (1996). *Hells Angels: A strange and terrible saga*. New York: Random House.

Thompson, H. S. (1999). *Hells Angels: A strange and terrible saga*. New York: Modern Library.

Thompson, T. (2009). *Gangs: A journey into the heart of the British underworld*. London: Hodder and Stoughton.

Trethewy, S., and Katz, T. (1998). *Motorcycle gangs or motorcycle mafia*. http://www.ncjrs.gov/app/publications.

Winterhalder, E. (2005). *Out in bad standing: Inside the Bandidos Motorcycle Club: The making of a worldwide dynasty*. Owasso, OK: Blockhead City Press.

http://www.woai.com/most popular/story.asp?/content-id-d3e0dce-483a-9424-fb66fi3a6260.

Suggested Reading

Harley Riders Ireland. n.d. *History*. http://homepage.tinet.ie/~rockedge/hri/history.htm.

Chapter 4

Serial Murder

Introduction

Perhaps no single type of murder has become so popular in the media and on America's mind than that of serial murder. These killers have become cultural icons and their names have become as famous as the entertainers who portray them in movies or on television. By the same token, the authors who write of their exploits have become famous and rich. If you are interested in the topic of serial murder, you certainly know the names of the crime authors, whether the cases are true or works of fiction. We know Anne Rule, the former friend and covolunteer at a rape crisis center with Ted Bundy. Rule volunteered with Bundy at the rape crisis center with Bundy as he was an intern majoring in psychology at the University of Washington in Seattle. From her experiences and interactions with Bundy, she developed a relationship with him over the years until he was arrested and placed on trial in Florida. Her book, *The Stranger Beside Me* (2009), made her rich and famous. Rule is a friend of ours. We like her. From the beginnings as a writer for true-crime magazines, she has gone on to write books about other famous killers, including Randy Woodfield, *The I-5 Killer* (Stack, 1984); Jerry Brudos, *The Lust Killer* (Stack, 1983a); Harvey Carignan, *The Want-Ad Killer* (Stack, 1983b); and Diane Downs, *Small Sacrifices* (Rule, 1987). Rule is an icon in her field and deserves to be so.

Another friend of ours is Thomas Harris. His books are works of "fiction," partly based on facts of blended serial killers and part out of his own mind. *Red Dragon* (1981), *The Silence of the Lambs* (1988), *Hannibal* (2005), *Hannibal Rising* (2006), and others take the reader into a frightening world of make-believe of murder, cannibalism, heights of sufferings, and the absolute lows of human despair, all from the mind of a man who appears on the outside as mild-tempered, meek, and without a violent fiber in his entire body. Harris is a man who loves to eat fine foods and drink exotic wines, travel, and is kind to our grandkids. But his characters are straight from hell: Francis Dolarhyde and, of course, Hannibal Lecter. Even his victims sometimes are hard to feel sympathy for: Freddie Lounds, a sleazy reporter from a *National Enquirer*-type magazine, and Jack Crawford, who uses Clarice Starling and William Graham to do his work for him. Will Graham wants to come out of retirement from the FBI to work again on the case of Dr. Lecter. And Dr. Chilton, the head administrator at the hospital that houses Dr. Lecter, who tried to put the move on Clarice as she attempted to get his approval to interview Lecter at the request of Crawford. Finally, Dr. Hannibal Lecter, the "true psychopath" as Dr. Chilton has judged him to be. We see true evil in the eyes and face of Lecter as he "plays" his demented mind games with Clarice.

We have seen "true evil" personally. I have seen it on death row at San Quentin when I looked into the face of Douglas David Clark, the Hollywood Strip Killer. He admitted killing three scores of young women, decapitating their bodies, then placing human heads into his refrigerator. I shall never forget the way he crushed a paper drinking cup that had been once filled with a soda, throwing it onto the floor, and declaring that he gave that as much thought as he did crushing the life out of a young woman once he started his stalking process that would inevitably lead to her death. (Read *Murder Most Rare* [Kelleher, 1998] for a complete story of his murders along with his accomplice, Carol Bundy.) I have looked into the eyes of Ted Bundy on death row in Florida when he spoke of the killings of young women at the Chi Omega Sorority House on Super Bowl Sunday in 1978. I have seen from a short distance Charles Manson; and Angelo Buono, The Hillside Stranger, who along with his cousin Kenneth Bianchi, killed at least twenty-three women in Los Angeles. I have seen the anguish in the eyes of police detectives who could not solve the cases in time to save other young people's lives. I have sat in Oregon State Prison and listened to a man tell me that he had killed "ten score plus two," and then went into detail of one of his first murders when he was 18 and his victim was 16.

We have been sued by Randy Woodfield and Gerald Schaeffer for writing about them and calling them serial killers. Both suits failed to go to trial. With Woodfield, I cannot call him a serial killer (Stack, 1984), I can only say he is an "alleged" serial killer. Schaeffer's suit was dismissed. He later died of a beating in prison in Florida. What Schaeffer refused to acknowledge was that I was writing about a serial killer who killed in the Northeast, not in Florida (Ginsburg, 1990).

Initial Distinction of Serial Killers

According to Holmes and Holmes (2010) the initial distinction to be made concerning serial murder is geographical mobility. For example, there are some serial killers who live in an area, kill in that area, and remain in that area. John Wayne Gacy,

Richard Angelo, and Jeffrey Dahmer are all excellent examples of *geographically stable* serial killers. On the other hand, Ted Bundy, Eddie Leonski, and Michael Swango are examples of *geographically transient* serial killers who travel far distances to kill and dispose of their victims. Bundy killed in eleven states; Swango killed in several states and foreign countries over an extended period of time; and Leonski, a private in the military during WWII, killed five people in different areas of Australia. He was arrested by the local authorities and hanged by the American military.

Types of Serial Killers

Holmes and DeBurger (1988) developed a typology of serial killers cited by other researchers and authors across the world. Holmes and DeBurger note four types of serial killers: visionary, mission, hedonistic, and power/control.

Visionary Serial Killer

The visionary is the kind of serial killer who is typically psychotic. He hears voices or sees visions. The visions or voices command he kill. A good example of a visionary killer is Joseph Kallinger. Kallinger said a head would float into a room and he was commanded to kill. Following the directions of the head, Charlie, Kallinger first killed his son, then three other people until he was caught (Schreiber, 1983). Kallinger was caught by the police and later sent to a hospital for the criminally insane where he died of natural causes.

Mission Serial Killer

The mission serial killer murders "bad people." Who are the bad people? Whomever the mission killer defines as such. Witness the case of Beoria Simmons. Simmons was a 28-year-old black male who had a white girlfriend. His girlfriend broke up with him and started dating another man. Simmons started killing white females with reddish-brown hair. He first shot 16-year-old Robin Barnes four times, one time in the neck, once in the back, and two times in the chest. This killing was followed by the murder of 27-year-old Shannon House. She was shot one time in the neck. The third victim was Nancy Bettman, 39. All three victims were abducted at gunpoint in the early morning hours. They were all white and all had reddish-brown hair. Simmons stated that "nice girls" are not out on the streets at 3 a.m., so they must be prostitutes. None were. He stated that he could not understand why people were upset with him; all he was doing was getting rid of sexually transmitted diseases in Louisville, Kentucky. Simmons is now serving a life sentence in Kentucky (Holmes and Holmes, 2010).

Hedonistic Serial Killer

The hedonistic serial killer murders for pleasure. There are three subtypes of this type of serial killer: the lust killer, the thrill killer, and the comfort killer. The lust killer usually murders fueled by a sexual fantasy. The rituals are closely followed and each time the killer attempts to realize his ultimate goal. This fantasy is explained in this story told to us in a western state prison:

> Five hours. Five long hours have passed and I still don't have a damn thing to show for my time and efforts. Off to the left I can see the sun beginning to descend behind the dirty gray hills. And the thought of this is so infuriating to me that I smash my fist down hard upon the thinly padded surface of my plastic dashboard as if this eruption of pointed violence could somehow exorcize the demon that was threatening to confuse me from within. I was feeling betrayed. Once again the wills of the female bitch had defeated me. After all, I am the ultimate man. The very epitome of power and glory. And she, as all shes, is a nothing.
>
> I am nearing my suburban hometown, and then all of a sudden I can see her standing by the side of the road, her right arm extended from her body and her thumb in an upright position. Blond-haired, blue-eyed, unmistakably young, very definitely female, cheerleader type.
>
> I could barely contain myself in my seat as I thought what I had in store for her if she would only get into my car. Thank God I had my seatbelt on. Good old-fashioned sex, rape, and then merciful murder if she will only get into my car. I pulled onto the shoulder of the road and depressed my brake pedal until my car came to a complete stop. I looked into my rear view mirror and saw her running toward me, incidentally jiggling in all the right places. She poked her head into the passenger side of my car of which I had already rolled the window almost all the way down.
>
> "Hi," she said. "My name is Becky. Can you give me a lift to the Fashion Place Mall?"
>
> I was pleasantly surprised by her stated destination because the Fashion Place Mall was not far from where I lived, and this would make it easier to exercise my drug lure.
>
> "Oh, the Fashion Place Mall is not far from where I live. Hop on inside little girl, looks like you found the right taxi."
>
> She opened the passenger side door and settled herself in the seat. I decided to play some mind games with the young girl to my right.
>
> I asked, "How old are you? 15? 16?"
>
> I could see her chest with a sense of self-importance as she thought that I thought that she was actually older than what she was.

"No," she responded. "I am 14. I am a sophomore at Thomas Jefferson School."

"Boy, you sure look older than that."

Again, I could see her chest swell, and I was pleased.

We continued our trip up the I-5 expressway. I asked her, "Do you and your friends ever smoke any pot at school?"

I pulled out a small plastic bag loaded with marijuana and held it over by the rear view mirror so she could see it.

She looked at me quizzically and asked, "You're not a cop, are you?"

"No," and I laughed. "I'm anything but a cop. Look in my glove compartment. I have some cigarette papers in there."

After she rummaged through the contents of the glove compartment looking for the papers that I knew were not there, she looked over her shoulder toward me.

"Oh, that's right. A friend of mine was at the house last night, and we changed tires on our cars. I think he left the papers on my workbench. Why don't you come home with me"?

She ran my words around in her brain. Should she or should she not? It was her decision. If she does she dies. If not, she lives to see another sunset.

And she said, "Are you sure you can get me to the mall on time"?

I looked at my watch. It was 7:20. "What time do you have to meet them?" I asked.

"8 o'clock," she replied.

"You have plenty of time." Yes, she had plenty of time to die. It would be a while before the truth comes crashing down upon her, but she has plenty of time to die.

For the first time that evening I pulled onto the driveway of my suburban hometown. By design I depressed the round red button on top of my garage door opener, and my garage door went up with a heavy moan. Noiselessly and silently, I pulled into my garage and gently depressed the brake pedal until my car came to a complete stop. I depressed the red button again, and my garage door slammed shut with a heavy thud. In the dark and murky silence of my garage. A small feminine voice to my right demanded, "Hey, mister, what are you doing?"

I now had no need in maintaining a continuing charade. I lashed out with my balled up right fist and hit her in her stomach. With a loud whoosh, all the breath came out of her lungs. I quickly and efficiently moved out of my seat and sat on her lap with my knees on either side of her legs. By design I reached under the seat and pulled out a short rope that I tied around her wrists. Also by design I reached out from under the seat and pulled out another small piece of rope. With this I tied her ankles together. Then from my front pocket I pulled two handkerchiefs, one I rolled into a ball and put it in her mouth, the other I blindfolded her. Then, by design, I pulled out a knife from my rear left pocket. I pulled her head back by her hair, placed the edge of the knife to her throat and said, "Pay attention, slut. One false move and you're gonna be dead! Got that?"

As best she could with my hand holding her as I was, she nodded up and down. I sat back in my seat, smoked a cigarette, and let the smoke over towards her so she would know what I was doing. All the while she crying and sobbing. But I did not care. She, by now, was a nothing. She was nothing more than a doll. She had no parents, no siblings, and no friends. She also would not suffer from what I had planned for her, she had no feelings.

After I finished my cigarette, I put it out on the concrete floor of my garage with the heel of my shoe and walked around the front of my car with the knife in my right hand. I opened the passenger door with my left a hand and pulled her out by the hair on her head. I slammed her up against the back fender, put the knife to her throat and said, "Remember what I told you. One false move and you're gonna be dead! Got that?"

She again shook her head up and down.

I turned my head toward the small door in my garage that would lead down the hall, past the kitchen then into the bedroom where everything was ready for little Ms. Becky. Then all hell broke loose. The bitch ran from me. Despite being blindfolded and hobbled, she ran from me. She ran into the lowered garage door and fell to the floor. With her bound feet she started to kick the door, making a terrible din. My neighbors are going to hear; they are going to call the police. I'm gonna get caught.

I ran toward her and tripped over my feet. The knife came out of my hand and fell under the car. I got down on knees and fumbled around the area but to no avail. Convinced I could not find my keys, I stood up and ran toward her with my lower right shoulder and as she too was starting to rise. I ran into the small of her back and sent her crashing onto a pile of weightlifting machines that I had mounted in the corner of the garage. A weight fell onto her neck and made an awful, crunching sound. I carried this worthless piece of female trash over my shoulder and walked out of my garage, down the hallway, and into the room. I carried her over to my closet, opened the door and deposited Ms. Becky onto the floor. I then went back to my kitchen, looked out my window to see if my neighbors had been alerted to any of the noise she had made, and when I was convinced none had, I opened my refrigerator and drink a beer in one long gulp. And then I went back into my bedroom. Yes everything was ready for little Ms. Becky. On one wall was a full-length mirror where she would take off all of her skin-tight clothing that she wears and shows off so brightly. On the bed, snaking from each end of the mattress, was a heavy leather belt that would hold her down while she received her just desserts. On the table next to the bed were tools that would assist in her punishment: rough-tooth metal clips, a handheld lamp with a scorching hot light bulb, a pair of pliers, a pair of needle-nosed pliers, rough grit sandpaper, and as an added twist, a small container of mace which women like to spray in the face of their male superiors.

I walked over to my closet door. I slid open the lock that was mounted on the outside of the door. My right hand raised if she were stupid enough to resist me again, I opened the door until a tiny bit of light shone upon her as she was upon my floor. She was still, much too still. I noted a small drop of blood on her upper left thigh, and she was a pasty white color, and her head lay motionless upon her left breast. And she was dead. She was dead.

The thought of that was so infuriating to me that I pulled her out of my closet by her hair, and threw her upon my bed. I beat her one minute, raped her the moment after that, and kicked her seemingly with no transition between the attacks. Finally when near exhaustion made it impossible for me to go on any longer, I pulled away from the worthless piece of female meat and went into my kitchen. I drank five beers and ate huge gobs of food. But neither the food nor the alcohol could satisfy this urgent, eating feeling. I needed another piece of female meat and I needed it tonight.

Barely an hour had passed, and for the second time that evening I pulled my car onto my driveway of my suburban hometown. I depressed that round, red light, and my garage door opened with a moan, and then I depressed my brake pedal. The garage door slammed shut, and inside the sudden and murky darkness of my garage a small feminine voice demanded to know, "Hey, mister, what are you doing"?

I had not returned empty-handed.

Tonight I ate the female meal.

I slept well that night.

This killer murdered for sexual reasons and also committed acts of necrophilia.

Jerry Brudos is a good example of a lust killer; sex becomes the primary motivation. He was the killer of four young women in Spokane, Washington, and Salem, Oregon. After he killed his first victim he cut off her ankle and used it as a visual aphrodisiac. For ten months that was pleasurable enough. However, he felt the need to kill again, and this time he cut the breasts off his second victim. When he made molds of the breasts, the molds fell apart. With his third victim, he cut off her breasts too, but this time he put more hardener into the epoxy mold and her breasts were placed on either end of the mantle in his living room. His fourth victim's body was not visually appealing to Jerry; he hanged her in the garage, and send bolts of electricity to make her jump. Jerry had some form of sex with each victim after they were dead (Stack, 1983a).

For the thrill serial killer, the motivation to kill is sexual. However, what separates the lust killer from the thrill killer is that the latter needs the victim to be alive when the torture, sexual violence, and any mutilation occurs.

The thrill killer feeds off the display of fear from the victim. The thrill killer is modeled after Ken Bianchi and Angelo Buono, the Hillside Stranglers. Both captured their victims, tortured them while they alive, and disposed of them after they were deceased. In other words, after the victims were dead, the excitation was over (O'Bryan, 1985).

The comfort killer, usually a female, murders for creature comfort reasons: money, insurance, or business interests. Aileen Wuornos is an example. Traveling and hitchhiking on the highways in Florida, Wuornos killed seven men, then robbed them. She stole money, personal effects, cars, and other material things. Sex was not a motivating factor (Reynolds, 2003).

> I don't particularly enjoy killing, you know, I enjoy the stalk, the planning, and the hunt much more.
>
> **—Richard Kuklinski, serial killer (as quoted in Carlo, 2006, 3)**

Richard Kuklinski is another example of a comfort-type serial killer. Born in 1935, Kuklinski grew up in a poor section of Jersey City, New Jersey, with a mother who was emotionally cold and a father who was abusive. Educated in Catholic schools, Kuklinski dropped out before completing high school. Faced with a future of menial jobs with low pay, Kuklinski got a job with the New York and New Jersey crime mobs as a hit man. Kuklinski admits to more than twenty hits for the mob over a thirty-year period (Carlo, 2006). He was a killer who relied on many different ways to kill people. He would beat people to death, poison others, and would use any method his client would demand. For example, one client demanded that the victim suffer before he died. Kuklinski abducted the man at gunpoint, took him to a cave where there were hundreds of rats. Kuklinski tied the man down with rope and duct tape, videotaped the rats eating the man thereby killing him (Carlo, 2006, 5–7). As proof of his successful job, he showed the videotape to his client who was well pleased.

> When my father—father, that's a joke—came home and I said "hello," he'd say hello by slapping me across the face.
>
> **—Richard Kuklinski, serial killer (as quoted in Carlo, 2006, 16)**

Eventually Kuklinski was apprehended by the police and in 1986 started to serve a life sentence for the murder of five men. He died of natural causes in prison of 2005. His wife, Barbara, divorced him while he was in prison. They had three children, two girls and a boy.

Power/Control Serial Killer

The power/control serial killer is motivated by the complete possession of the victim. As Ted Bundy said in a personal interview in September 1987, while on death row in Florida, he killed and possessed the victims like "a potted plant or a Porsche." Jeffrey Dahmer stated that killing his victims was all about possessing his victims. That was why he wanted them to be his slaves and he tried to turn them into zombies (personal interview, 1987). He drilled holes in their heads to attempt to turn them into his willing slaves to become his sexual servants and do whatever he wanted them to do.

> The Law, alone and aloof by its very nature, has no access to the emotions that might justify murder.
>
> **—Marquis de Sade**

How Many Serial Killers Are There?

There is no way to correctly determine the exact number of serial killers extant in the United States today. The estimates range from 30 to well over 200. We really only know about the number of serial killers by examining the number of unsolved homicides as well as the number of known serial killers currently under arrest and in correctional facilities. In our travels across the nation offering homicide investigation seminars, we have become aware of cases that the local authorities believe are related due to forensic evidence. The numbers are higher in states such as Florida and Texas than in states such as Kentucky and North Dakota. Nonetheless in every jurisdiction we have visited, the local police have asked us about homicide cases they believe may be related.

History of Serial Murder in the United States

It has been traditionally stated that America's first serial killer was H. H. Mudgett (a.k.a. H. W. Holmes) who allegedly killed close to one hundred men and women in the Chicago area at the close of the 19th century. However, there were other serial killers before this time. Billy the Kid and Doc Holiday were both serial killers but killed for different reasons than the traditional serial killer who kills for sexual pleasure (Holmes and Holmes, 2010).

A rise in serial killers occurred in the 1960s and 1970s when apparently was coined by Dr. Donald Lunde in California (Lunde, 1976). Killers such as Edmund Kemper, Jerry Brudos, Ken Bianchi, and Angelo Buono became infamous icons of the evil that existed in the world. In a study by Hickey (2005), he mentioned that in his research he found that there were 558 serial killers in the United States since 1900 (Hickey, 2005). These are the numbers of predators. How about the number of victims? Hickey reported that the victims of these 558 could be as many as 5,560 victims. There is no way to determine exactly the number of victims, and the reader should be aware that these are only estimates. As American society moved into the 1980s, the increase in the number of victims to serial killers, and the apparent increase in serial murder accompanied the increase in the apparent rise of violent crime. But this was due to is more than an increase in the reporting of serial murder and the sophistication in the reporting of such crimes. There arose a pandemic fear in the minds of many that everyone was at risk of falling a victim to a serial killer.

What is the real story? The Justice Department report stated that between 1,190 and 1,760 Americans were slain by serial killers, or about 120 to 180 a year during the peak years of the 1980s. Jack Levin, a professor of criminal justice at Northeastern University in Boston, estimates that there are about 20 serial killers accounting for 200 victims a year in the United States. Ann Rule, an expert in serial murder, estimates there are about 300 such predators lurking "just below our level of awareness." So, the numbers range from 20 to 5,000 serial killers and victims.

However, perhaps what we should know is that we should not confuse numbers with serious and human suffering. Twenty serial killers are too many. Five thousand serial victims are too many. We should not confuse the serious of the crime and the number of victims.

Theories of Serial Murder

How and why some people become a serial killer is unknown. But this does not keep some from theorizing. Is it "bad genes," somatotypes, social learning, or bad experiences as a child? From the perspective of the serial killers themselves in our interviews, they too have no idea. Bundy told us in the interview that he had no idea why he became a serial killer. It was not the pornography that he saw early in his life. It may have provided him with some ideas about committing the crime, for example, cannibalism.

Holmes and Holmes (2010) developed a theory of fractured identity. In this theory, it is suggested that something very early in a child's life occurred that left the child with a very painful experiences and a psyche fractured that has never fully healed. With Ted Bundy it could have been the occasion of him learning that his sister Louise was actually his mother and that he was born out of wedlock. With Henry Lucas it could have been being made to watch his mother having sex with other men in a prostitution situation. With Edmund Kemper, it may have been the blow to the head he received as a preadolescent. Witness the testimony of Manny C:

I believe that my own rise to serial murder came from the "Great Banana Episode." I think I was 6 years old at the time. My father, an abusive sort, informed me that the sole banana that remained on the kitchen countertop that night was his, and he would have it with his morning breakfast the next morning. I promised him I would not eat it. I went to bed that night, got up one time in the night to go to the bathroom and went back to bed.

The next morning when I went downstairs to the kitchen for breakfast. He was waiting for me. Someone had eaten the banana during the night, and Papa was convinced I had done so. He asked and I told him the truth. I had not eaten the banana. He was not satisfied with the truth and told me to stand in the corner until he got home later that afternoon after work. All day long I stood in the corner. I had to go to the bathroom, but my mother would not let me out of the corner in the kitchen because my corner, clean myself up, and get back into good standing with both my mother and dad was to lie. I learned the value of the lie. I could get anything I wanted just by lying. I told him that I got really hungry during the night and ate the banana. I also told him I was sorry and would never do something like that again. He was satisfied. I got out of the corner, and I got cleaned up. Everyone was now OK since I had lied. I learned the value of the lie.

SERIAL KILLER NICKNAME

Jerry Brudos, "The Shoe Fetish Killer"

Andreu (2005) stated that serial killers come from homes of pathology. Many had been physically abused as children as well as being victims of sexual abuse. They are motivated by obsessive deviant sexual desires and fantasies. Many also are very selective of their victims because the physical attributes of the victims bear some resemblance to people in their pasts.

Despite the basic etiology of the serial killer, they all appear to have some common traits or characteristics (Korte and Fahey, 2006):

■ Repetition
■ Lack of preexisting relationship with the victim
■ A compulsion to kill
■ Lack of an apparent motive

The critical question to ask is where do these items come from. Psychologists have for some time tried to examine the exact etiology of the serial killer. For example, Gray et al. (2003) report that the Implicit Association Tests (IATs) are used by psychologists to delve into the gap between the conscious and the unconscious mind. IATs have been used in legal circles to reveal unconscious discrimination on the grounds of race, religion, gender, age, and sexual orientation. One test has now been adapted to show that psychopathic murderers have abnormal cognitive associations regarding violence that may underpin violent acts. The tests results suggest there may be two distinct populations of psychopathic offenders: one with deficient social beliefs (and an increased disposition toward extreme violence) and the other in which such negative beliefs are absent.

Heredity and genetics also have a role to play. There is still a hunt for the "crime gene." The extra Y chromosome debate is still alive. Richard Speck, for example, was once thought to have the extra Y chromosome, and this would have purposively accounted for his bizarre and murderous activity. No evidence was found of the extra Y chromosome existence. The reaction to this "finding" would be to examine the general society and ascertain how many law-abiding citizens possess the extra Y chromosome and still do not become involve in crime, especially violent personal offenses. Johnson et al. (2004) suggest that genetic analysis is needed to more fully understand and appreciate the role biology plays in the formation of the personality from early life choices to the selection of a marriage partner and even to the exercise of other choices in one's life.

SERIAL KILLER NICKNAME

Angel Maturino Resendiz, "The Railroad Killer"

Despite the findings of some and the invalidated suggestions of others, there is no clear picture that biology plays the sole or principle role in the commission of serial murder. There are so few serial killers who have been biologically and physiologically tested to locate any one factor, be it the extra Y chromosome or a blow to the head, that would account for a serial killer mentality. Indeed, the lobes of the brain are necessary for mental development although the different lobes are responsible for differing mental processing (Stuss et al., 2001). The goal of this type of examination would be to distinguish if there is one particular part of the brain that could hold the responsibility for continuing fatal violence. Until a reliable sample can be obtained and tested, there is no scientific statement that can be made concerning the exact role of biology as a determining factor of a serial killer personality.

However, there is still no one explanation into the exact etiology of the serial killer. It may be that some are simply born with an innate predisposition toward personal violence. It may be inheritance or it may be social experiences, but it is more than likely a strange and unique combination of the two.

Holmes, Tewskbury, and Holmes report that in their study of serial killers, there is something that occurs in their preadolescence that causes a psychological break in their mental condition. With Bundy it could have been the discovery that he was illegitimate. But there are thousands of people who discover that they too are illegitimate. One author believes that a "blow to the head" when they are children also causes one to become a serial killer. It is also true many if not most young people received a blow to the head when they were children, and few become serial killers. The actual answer to the basic etiology of a serial killer is unknown. From the perspective of the serial killers themselves in our interviews, they too have no idea. As mentioned previously, Bundy told us in the interview that he had no idea why he became a serial killer. It was not the pornography that he saw early in his life. It may have provided him with some ideas about committing the crime, for example, cannibalism. But there were other things, too. Could it be the unique combination of the social environment and the genetic background of the children from their parents, grandparents, and others in the family? Bundy had brothers and sisters, none of whom are killers or criminals. Douglas Clark's father was a naval officer. We could list serial killer after serial killer all of whom had families with no major criminal record. Of course there are some killers who come from delinquent and criminal families. Charles Manson's mother allegedly was a prostitute and encouraged Charles to witness her business transactions (Bugliosi, 1975). We have already witnessed the home life of Richard Kuklinski. But there are others who came from less than desirable families but became socially law-abiding families.

In truth, there appears to be no one true and accurate item to account for the serial murderer mentality. It is a strange and unique combination of factors that uniquely occurs to a person; no other person undergoes the same experiences in the same sequence of events. For example, we have all gone to the first grade, the second grade, and so on. But each of us have had a different first-grade teacher, and no one was treated exactly the same in the first grade.

Organized versus Disorganized Serial Killers

No discussion of a psychological theory position would be complete without looking at the research done by the Federal Bureau of Investigation (FBI). On the surface, the typology of the organized and disorganized offender appears to be useful and theoretically comfortable. However, there is no way to validate the information purported by the FBI. The names of the killers interviewed or the instrument used to gather the information has never been disclosed. Originally termed the "organized nonsocial" and the "disorganized asocial," the terms were used to describe personality types of lust killers. The assumption was that all lust killers would be or become serial killers. Later the names were altered; the nonsocial and asocial labels were omitted. Perhaps because of the influence and pressure of the psychological and psychiatric communities, the labels organized and disorganized now refer to crime scenes.

One must be careful, however, to understand that the organized and disorganized labels do nothing to explain the basic etiology of the serial offender. This approach does nothing to examine the basic motivating factors in the behavior of the serial killer. It also does not attempt to explain the how or the why the person becomes a violent personality. What is does do, and it does appear to do this well, is to examine the crime-scene characteristics and then from that information describe the type of person who may have committed some crime.

As we examine the information offered by the FBI and others who are involved in criminal investigation assessment, or psychological profiling, it is apparent that there is some attention paid to the role of fantasy in the mind of the serial or lust killer (Burgess et al., 1986; Douglas and Olshaker, 1995). But how does the fantasy develop and what is the role of the fantasy in serial predation? This is never fully discussed to the satisfaction of many who are involved in the research of serial murder.

History of Serial Murder outside the United States

In the latter part of the 16th century, the Countess of Transylvania in Romania became a historical feature in the annals of serial murder. Elizabeth Bathory, born in 1560, became an inspiration for Bram Stoker's *Dracula*. In the course of her life she was thought to have killed as many as six hundred young and attractive women. The countess was obsessed with her skin beauty. Told by one of her consultants that the blood of virgins would rejuvenate her skin texture and beauty, she and several cohorts enticed young women from her Romanian village to come to her castle for educational sessions to become a member of the new middle and ruling class. A legend developed over the years that she would hang the young women nude over her bathtub to let their blood drain out of their bodies. She would bathe in the blood and drink the blood that would drain from their slit throats.

SERIAL KILLER PROFILE
Name: Elizabeth Bathory
Born: 1560
Died: 1614
Location: Hungary and Romania
Victims: About 600
Method: Strangulation and knifing
Punishment: Cell confinement until her death

Soon, the stories spread in the town, and she was arrested along with her accomplices. Since she was from royal blood, she could not stand trial for any crimes. While her accomplices were either executed or sent to prison for the rest of their lives, Bathory was confined to a small room in her castle, with only a small opening in a bricked wall. She died in 1614 after four years in her small room.

Did she really take baths in the blood of virgins? There is not total agreement on this. Some researchers believe this is only a legend. They believed she killed scores of young women, but it may be more of a sexual fantasy that centered on the torture and murder than the vampirism of drinking blood. They believe that she was introduced to flagellantism and enjoyed whipping the young women, nude, and on their breasts and faces as well as the genital areas. It was said that she enjoyed looking at the pain on the faces of the young women as they were tortured and killed. Whatever the actual truth, she was a serial killer. Her fantasies centered on vampirism and torture, watching death overcome the beautiful women in her kingdom.

But she is not the only serial killer in the early years. Giles de Rais was a compatriot of Joan of Arc. A nobleman, he was thought to have killed more than one hundred young boys. He would stab them in their throats and have sexual intercourse with that artificial orifice opening. The government and the church held him for trial and they found him guilty. He was decapitated and his head and body were buried in different parts of the countryside. Why? So he could never be resurrected.

In France, Helene Jegado was employed as a domestic servant. She was also a serial killer. Between 1833 and 1851, she poisoned at least twenty-three people. At the time of her first killing, she was 30 years old. If someone displeased her or was angry with her, she retaliated with poison. In 1851 she was arrested for the murder of one of her former employees. The investigators determined this death was strangely similar to the previous employee. At the trial, she was found to be guilty and sentenced to die by the guillotine. She was executed on February 26, 1852.

In Holland, Maria Catherina Swanenburg was convicted of killing twenty-seven people between 1880 and 1883. Interestingly she failed in her attempts to kill fifty more victims. The court decided not to execute her but to sentence her to life in a house of "correction" for the rest of her life. She died in prison in 1915 at the age of 75.

In Germany in the mid-1800s Karl Grossman, a butcher, was found guilty of four murders of women who visited his apartment in Berlin. Some believe he had killed as many as fifty women who came to his apartment, but were never seen leaving. Some suspected he butchered the remains of his victims and sold them at his butcher shop. He was convicted of murder and sentenced to death. However, before he could be executed, he was found dead. He had hanged himself. He was 58.

Not all of the early serial killers are apprehended, as is true of the modern-day serial killers. For example, a Hungarian serial killer, Béla Kiss, killed at least twenty-four women. Their bodies were found in oil drums after his land was searched by the local police after he had left to fight in the World War I. He strangled his victims. The police and the military searched for Kiss. When they went to his bed in his barracks, they found a corpse in his bed under the covers. He was never seen alive or dead after that. One police officer thought he had spotted him at Grand Central Station in New York City. However, Kiss vanished before he could be arrested by the authorities. His ultimate fate is unknown ("Béla Kiss," n.d.).

Karl Denke, a serialist from Germany, wrote the names of more than two dozen victims in his ledger. The police in addition found body parts and flesh in jars of pickling vinegar. He hanged himself in his cell on December 22, 1924, at the age of 54. A convicted serial killer, he was also a cannibal and there was some thought that he sold "meat products" to the local meat market. ("Karl Denke," n.d.).

Serial Killers in the United Kingdom

Perhaps one of the most well-known serial killers was Jack the Ripper. Jack killed in the Whitechapel area of London in 1888. Whitechapel was at the time a lower-class area of London, and many of the homeless, disenfranchised, and unemployed lived there. Many women had no other source of income and begged for food and money; others were prostitutes. The ruling and upper class of London seemed to have little awareness of the people of Whitechapel. Only with the murder of women that occurred in 1888 did a focus return to that part of one of the world's largest cities of the time.

SERIAL KILLER PROFILE
Name: Jack the Ripper
Number of Victims: 5–7
Location: London
Identity: Unknown
Date: 1888

The murders executed by Jack the Ripper commenced with the killing of Mary Ann Nichols on August 31, 1888. This was followed by Annie Chapman, September 8; Elizabeth Stride, September 30; Catharine Eddowes, September 30; and the last victim, Mary Jane Kelly, November 9. Then the murders stopped. The killings of these five victims progressed with violence and mutilation. Kelly's body (the only murder to occur inside a dwelling, the others occurred in the streets of Whitechapel) was disemboweled and otherwise mutilated (Whitehead and Rivett, 2006).

The identity of Jack remains unknown, although some believe he was George Chapman, who will be covered later in this chapter. Others are equally convinced that James Maybrick was Jack. Others are believers that Prince Albert Victor, Montague John Druitt, Dr. T. Neil Cream, or Lewis Carroll was Jack (Evans and Skinner, 2002). The FBI's Roy Hazelwood tried his hand as profiling the Ripper case. His profile was difficult to accept for many (Holmes and Holmes, 2001). Patricia Cornwell (2002) also tried her hand at psychological profiling as a crime fiction author. Her identification as to the true identity of Jack the Ripper can be debated by Ripperologists across the world especially since her "Jack" was in France during four of the five killings. Our profile of Jack the Ripper is:

- A white male
- Right-handed
- Well-dressed
- Lived near the Whitechapel area at the time of the killings
- Single or lived with disabled partner
- Self-employed
- Sexually dysfunctional, perhaps a preoperation transsexual
- Antisocial and difficult to be around
- Domineering
- Chronic masturbator
- Between 35 and 45 years of age
- Educated for his times

Offering a profile of Jack the Ripper is a safe project. This case will undoubtedly never be resolved. But nonetheless it remains one of the most famous of all cases of serial murder across the world.

John George Haigh was a serial killer from England. He was born in Yorkshire in 1909 and died in 1949. As a child in England, Haigh was raised in a very religious family, and as a child his father erected a fence around his yard. He was not allowed to go any further than ten feet from his fence. When he was 21, he was fired from his job as an engineer at a motorcar factory, and then went into other jobs as an insurance salesman and a clerk in an advertising firm. He was fired from his jobs for various reasons including stealing. Married at the age of 25, his marriage soon failed when he was sent to prison for business fraud. His wife left him when he was sent to prison, having his child while he was incarcerated. Moving to London after his second prison experience, for business fraud again, his dry cleaning business failed after his partner was killed in a motorcycle accident, Haigh was sent to prison again for four years for fraud again. Once released, he was jailed for theft.

Freed in 1944, Haigh developed a plan for murder. While in prison and later while working as an accountant for an engineering company, he experimented with mice to see how they would react after being dumped into a vat of sulfuric acid. Taking his scheme to another level, he dumped the body of William McSwan, a former employer, into the vat and then poured acid into the vat over his body. He stole McSwan's money and sold his business interests. Following this method with eight other victims, the police finally caught up Haigh. He was executed for his crimes on the gallows in 1949. Haigh's victims included (Ambler, 1964):

- William Donald McSwan, September 9, 1944
- Donald McSwan, July 3, 1945
- Amy McSwan, July 2, 1945
- Archibald Henderson, February 12, 1948
- Rosalie Henderson, February 12, 1948
- Olive Henrietta Robarts Durand-Deacon, February 18, 1949

Another "Ripper" case is the Yorkshire Ripper, Peter Sutcliffe. Born in England in 1946, he was known as a loner in school and left school at the age of 15. He worked at several jobs, usually low-paying positions including a grave digging position; he also had jobs as a truck driver, salesman, and an assembly line worker. He married in 1967. He killed his first victim in 1975. From 1975 until 1980, he killed thirteen victims, and assaulted but did not kill seven more. The methods of his murders included stabbing and beating with a hammer (Burn, 1984). He also wrote letters to the police taunting them with his crimes. After his arrest, Sutcliffe originally pled not guilty. He later changed his plea to guilty of manslaughter and seven counts of attempted murder. At the trial, Sutcliffe was found guilty of thirteen murders and was sentenced to life imprisonment with a recommendation that he serve at least 30 years. He is eligible for parole in 2011 (Bilton, 2003).

Team Killers

There are a few serial killers who kill with others. Angelo Buono and Kenneth Bianchi were the infamous Hillside Stranglers. Cousins, they killed mainly in Los Angeles area in the late 1970s. The numbers for this pair range from 10 to 20 young women, some were prostitutes (e.g., Yolanda Washington), but many were not. After abducting the young females, they often would take them home, rape them, and then kill them. After killing them they would dump them on the sides (the hills) of the expressway. Bianchi eventually moved to the state of Washington at the insistence of Buono where he killed again. Bianchi was caught in Washington and received a life sentence at Walla Walla State Prison (O'Brien, 1985). Buono was sentenced to life in prison in California. He died of a heart attack in 2002.

Fred and Rose West were another serial killer pair. Fred, born in 1941, was first married to Rena Costello in 1962. Rena was pregnant by another man they married. She later gave birth to a daughter, Charmaine. While still married, Fred met his soon-to-be second wife, Rose, when she was 15. At age 17, Rose gave birth to their daughter Heather. In 1972, Rose killed Rena and Fred killed Charmaine. Fred and Rose then had a second daughter, Mae. In the next several years, the couple killed more than ten victims, culminating in the murder of their daughter

Heather when she was 16 (Burn, 1998). In the course of the police investigation, the authorities determined that they killed, dismembered, and buried many of the bodies on their own premises. Fred was arrested and at one time confessed to murdering thirty people. He later recanted his confession and hanged himself in prison before his trial. Rose was charged with ten counts of murder; she was found guilty of all counts in 1995 and was given a life sentence (Bennett, 2005).

Another team of killers was Gerald and Charlene Gallego, a man and his mistress who thought she was his wife. Gerald had not bothered to get divorced from his previous wife (van Hoffman, 1990). He pair would abduct women in their van, Charlene would drive while Gerald would be in the back of the van raping and murdering the women. They murdered ten women around Sacramento, California, before they were caught. Charlene pled guilty to the murders and received a sixteen-year, nine-month sentence. Gerald was tried and convicted of murder and he received the death penalty. Charlene was released from prison in 1997. Gerald died in prison of cancer in 2002.

SERIAL TEAM KILLERS PROFILE

Names: Henry Lucas (1936–2001) and Ottis Toole (1947–1996)
Victims: Unknown, confessed to 300-plus, but that is likely an exaggeration
Locations: Across the U.S., Florida and Texas
Penalty: Death sentence, commuted to life

But perhaps one of the strangest of all team killers was that of Henry Lucas and Ottis Toole. Lucas said at one time that from 1960 to the mid-1980s, he and Toole committed more than 600 murders. He was given the death penalty because of the crimes and the number of the murders, but it was reduced by then–Governor George W. Bush to life in prison. In corresponding with Lucas over a period of several years, he could not read or write. Letters from author Ronald Holmes were answered by a nun who had befriended him. Lucas died of heart failure in prison on 2001 at the age of 64. Toole was sent to prison in Florida and confessed to three murders and later admitted to four more. Toole was an alleged homosexual, a cross dresser, and a pyromaniac; he died in prison in 1996 of liver failure (Hickey, 2005; personal communication, July 2009).

Colin Ireland declared as a New Year's resolution to become a serial killer. He is known in England to be the Gay Slayer since he killed gay men. He declared himself to be a mission-type serial killer because he was going to get rid of the "gay problem" in England. After his arrest, he was charged with five murders of gay men. He confessed to all five killings in 1983 and was given five life sentences (Ressler and Shachtman, 1998).

Of course, not all cases of serial murder in the United Kingdom are solved. In London from 1964 to 1965 there were several killings of young women from the ages of 21 to 30. The police are convinced these killings were all committed by the same person: there have been notes written, the last six victims were choked to death by oral sex, and the removal of teeth of four of the victims. This unknown killer is known as Jack the Stripper. Will this case ever be solved? Maybe not. The last killing was over forty years ago. One suspect killed himself, and since that time no other young women has been murdered in a similar manner.

Conclusion

There is no end in sight of the violence committed by strangers upon strangers in the world today. The cases multiply as time passes and there appears to be no end to their crimes of almost perfect, personal violence. The names of the killers become cultural icons. Books, movies, and television documentaries are made of the crimes and times. We remember their names but cannot recall the names of the victims. Of Bundy's victims, for example, how many names do we know? Or the victims of Henry Lucas, Ottis Toole, Jeffrey Dahmer? They each have a place in history, but they, and their sufferings, are invisible and hidden. Only the most violent have captured the attention of the populace and ensured their place in societies' consciousness for many years to come. Witness the case of Jack the Ripper. Mention him and then mention Mary Kelley. Hardly anyone knows the identity of Mary Kelley. How about Georgeann Hawkins, a victim of Ted Bundy? Did you know who she was before you read this book? Not many did.

Perhaps it is the nature of personal violence that captures a central place in our minds while we forget the recipient of that violence. We do not understand the violent personality; it is beyond our limited minds. We are fascinated, yet repelled by the atrocious acts committed by that person who wrecks havoc on the people who are undeserving of such violence. Perhaps also we recognized that it could also happen to us, the ordinary and responsible people of others' rights and privacy. Do we not then admire the powerful and neglect the powerless? This is an important item to examine and try to understand.

Discussion Questions

1. Discuss any serial killers that you might believe are crossover types.
2. Discuss the main traits of the main types of serial killers and how they are different from one type to the other.
3. What are the main differences between the organized crime scene and the disorganized crime scene?

4. Pick one serial killer we have not discussed in this chapter and profile the killer.
5. Delineate the differences between the organized and disorganized killers.

References

Ambler, E. (1964). *The ability to kill.* London: Four Square.
Andreu, N. (2005). *Serial killers: A homicide detective's take. Law Enforcement Technology* 23(2): 88, 90, 92, 94, 95.
Bennett, J. (2005). *The Cromwell Street murders: The detective's story.* New York: Sutton.
Béla Kiss. (n.d.). www.answers.com/topic/b-la-kiss.
Bilton, G. (2003). *Wicked beyond belief: The hunt for the Yorkshire Ripper.* London: Trafalgar Square.
Bugliosi, V. (1975). *Helter skelter: The true story of the Manson murders.* New York: Norton Press.
Burn, G. (1984). *Somebody's husband.* London: Heinemann Press.
Burn, J. (1998). *Happy like murderers.* London: Faber and Faber.
Carlo, P. (2006). *The ice man: Confessions of a mafia contract killer.* New York: St. Martin's Press.
Cornwell, P. (2002). *Portrait of a killer: Jack the Ripper case closed.* New York: G.P. Putnam.
Douglas, J., and Olshaker, M. (1995). *The mind hunter.* New York: Scribner Books.
French, W. (1991). *Bodies of evidence.* New York: Carol Publishing Group.
Ginsburg, P. (1990). *The shadow of death: The hunt for a serial killer.* New York: Charles Scribner's Sons.
Gray, N., Macculloch, M., Smith, J., Morris, M., and Snowden, R. (2003). Forensic psychology: Violence viewed by psychopathic murderers. *Nature* 423: 497–498.
Harris, T. (1981). *Red dragon.* New York: Putnam Press.
Harris, T. (1988). *Silence of the lambs.* New York: St. Martin's Press.
Harris, T. (2005). *Hannibal.* New York: Dell Books.
Harris, T. (2006). *Hannibal rising.* New York: Delacorte Press.
Hickey, E. (2005). *Serial murderers and their victims.* Belmont, CA: Wadsworth.
Holmes, R., and DeBurger, J. (1988). *Serial murder.* Thousand Oaks, CA: Sage.
Holmes, R., and Holmes, S. (2001). *Murder in America,* 2nd ed. Thousand Oaks, CA: Sage.
Holmes, R., and Holmes, S. (2010). *Serial murder,* 3rd ed. Thousand Oaks, CA: Sage.
Johnson, W., McGue, M., Krueger, R., and Bouchard, T. (2004). Marriage and personality: Agenetic analysis. *Social Problems* 86(2): 285–294.
Karl Denke. (n.d.). answers.com/topic/karl-denke.
Korte, R., and Fahey, S. (2006). Serial murder. In *Different crimes different countries: Understanding, treating, and preventing criminal behavior,* ed. D. Layton, L. O'Neill, et al., 207–230. Cincinnati, OH: Anderson Publishing Co.
Lunde, D. (1976). *Murder and madness.* San Francisco, CA: San Francisco Book Co.
O'Brien, D. (1985). *Two of a kind: The hillside stranglers.* New York: New American Library.
Ressler, R., and Shachtman, T. (1998). *I have lived in the monster.* New York: St. Martin's.
Reynolds, M. (2003). *Dead ends: The pursuit, conviction, and execution of female serial killer Aileen Wournos, the damsel of death.* New York: St. Martin's True Crime Library.
Rule, A. (1987). *Small sacrifices.* New York: New American Library.
Rule, A. (2009). *The stranger beside me.* New York: Pocket Books.
Schreiber, F. (1983). *The shoemaker.* New York: Signet.
Stack, A. [A. Rule]. (1983a). *The lust killer.* New York: Signet.

Stack, A. [A. Rule]. (1983b). *The want-ad killer*. New York: Signet.
Stack, A. [A. Rule]. (1984). *The I-5 killer*. New York: Signet.
Stuss, D., Gallup, G., and Alexander, M. (2001). The frontal lobes are necessary for the theory of mind. *Brain* 124: 279–286.
van Hoffman, E. (1990). *A venom in the blood*. New York: Donald Fine.

Suggested Reading

Larke, E. (2003). *The devil in the white city*. New York: Random House.
Myers, W., Gooch, E., and Meloy, J.R. (2005). Role of psychopathy and sexuality in a female serial killer. *Journal of Forensic Sciences* 50(3): 652–657.
Quinet, K. (2007). The missing: Toward a quantification of serial murder victimization in the United States. *Homicide Studies* 11(4): 318–339.

Chapter 5

Vampires and Cannibals

Introduction

When one thinks of vampires and cannibals, images come to mind of Bela Lugosi, Christopher Lee, Vincent Price, and other film stars of the horror genre portraying Dracula, the Wolf Man, or other monsters of the day. We do not consider modern-day human vampires who drink blood and kill for sexual reasons. Nor do we think of cannibals such as Ted Bundy, Ed Gein, and Richard Carpenter. We think not only of the movie versions, but also of Anne Rice's books and of Tom Cruise in the film, *Interview with the Vampire*; and others like it. But vampires have been with us since recorded history. Their stories of murder, bloodlust, and a search for immortality carry over from one time to another and from one society to another. Ancient Assyria literature acknowledged the existence of vampires. The Chinese, the Arabians, and many cultures of early Africa tell stories of vampires within their histories and folklores. Cannibals have been a part of mankind since the caveman days. The world of the gypsies is sated with stories and characters of vampires and cannibals.

What Is a Vampire?

Human beings have practiced blood drinking for many reasons throughout history, but drinking blood alone does not indicate that a person is a vampire. Only real vampires can directly absorb the energy in fresh blood, and for this reason some unfeigned vampires are attracted to blood and attain different ways of obtaining it. However, it is a rare vampire who cannot absorb energy in much more subtle ways (McNally and Florescu, 1994).

The Vampire

From where do vampires come from? Beliefs vary. Some are victims of vampires and later become vampires themselves. Others come from a dog or cat that crosses over a dead body or its grave. Others vampires are caused by someone casting a spell over another person. And it is not only humans that become vampires. Pumpkins, melons, and other fruits are left out in the open for a certain period of time, as well as horses, sheep and other animals accursed by witches and warlocks can turn into vampires or cannibals. In Russian folklore, vampires were said to have once been witches or people who had rebelled against the church while they were alive (Barber, 1988). Of course, in the Salem witch hunts in 1692 the early American colonies put many witches to death because the Bible in Exodus states, "Thou shalt not suffer a witch to live" (22:18), and Leviticus holds "A man also or woman that hath familiar spirit or that is a wizard, shall surely be put to death; they shall stone them with stones; their blood shall be upon them" (20:27). In 1591, King James of Scotland in 1591 authorized the torture of suspected witches in Scotland. England executed its last witch in 1682 (Linder, 2005). Some witches are believed to be able to turn into vampires, others into warlocks and cannibals (Kittredge, 1929).

What protects a potential victim from a vampire? Some believe holy water sprayed upon the cursed one; mirrors, crosses, or crucifixes; iron shavings and other metal products strategically placed around a room; or fruits and other food products, especially garlic, can deter a vampire.

One other deterrent to vampires that many are unaware of is that vampires cannot do harm in someone's abode unless they are invited inside at least once before. Casting seeds was another manner in which to protect one from vampires, the thought being that vampires would count each seed and become so involved and distracted, they would lose track of time and be suddenly caught by the sunlight. The rays of the sun, the light, would immediately disintegrate the vampire. Vampires are "night people" on a biochemical level. They have inverted circadian rhythms, with body cycles such as temperature peaks, menstrual onset, and the production of sleep hormones in the brain occurring at the opposite time of day from most people (Summers, 1980).

If caught, it was thought that vampires can be killed by decapitation, a wooden stake driven through its heart, or exposing it to sunlight. Other ways included touching it with a cross; or stealing the left sock, filling it with rocks, and throwing it into the river. Perhaps one of the most unusual but reliable manners to kill a vampire was the hiring of a professional hit man, a dhampir, the child of a vampire who could see both visible and invisible vampires.

Modern-day vampires are more immune to the physical dangers than the vampires of old. Garlic, crosses, holy water, and even sunlight do not seem to hold potential dangers as they did previously (Frost, 1989). In a new TV series, *The Vampire Diaries*, vampires walk the streets of a large city no longer fearful of the sunlight. They are depicted as demons and devils, something that was certainly missing in the original Bram Stoker novel. They are also seen in some instances as benevolent creatures greatly misunderstood but still with the need and compulsion to drink human blood.

The Rise in Popularity of Vampires

Bram Stoker (1897) awoke the interest of the populace with the story of Count Dracula, a vampire from Transylvania, the "land behind the clouds." Presumably his work was based in part on the story of Vlad Tepes (1431–1476), a warrior and regal character in Romania of the 15th century. As the Prince of Wallachia, he was a sadistic medieval character that would impale his enemies after victorious battles. Thus his nickname, Vlad the Impaler. The personal life of Vlad is unclear. Some stories claim that Vlad was beheaded by his enemies. Other sources state that he died an embittered individual; his wife, Elisabeta, had left him and committed suicide by jumping into a river. After being converted to Catholicism, Vlad renounced his faith because the Catholic priest told him that she could never enter heaven since she had taken her own life. He violently plunged his sword into a concrete statue and blood rushed out. The blood filled the apse of the church (Dundes, 1998).

There are other stories concerning the rise of Dracula. Another story has Vlad as a vampire accompanied by Mina Harker, his vampire partner. He changes her into a vampire so they will be able to live together forever as he and Elisabtha were to do. In a hunting accident, Dracula has his throat cut, and Mina knifes him to death. His body back to his original human form. Mina also changes since she is released from his vampire status upon the death of Dracula (Dundes, 1998).

As time passed, the image of the vampire has changed. The bat, for example, has emerged as a symbol for the vampire. We have all seen the bat flying though a darkened castle window with the moon reflected in the sky. The bat settles into the room and suddenly develops into a full human being, dressed in black with a cape flowing over his shoulders. He advances to a beautiful woman who both welcomes yet fears of his advances. As he smiles, his teeth grow and as she turns her head toward the camera, she grimaces with pain as his cuspids penetrate her neck and drains and drinks her blood.

But Vlad still is the "living" example of Dracula the vampire. Vlad was the son of Vlad Dracula and Princess Cneajna Moldavia. He had an older brother, Mircea, and a younger brother, Radu the Handsome. His family lived at the time in Transylvania. When Vlad was 26, his father and brother Mircea were both killed by the Ottomans. Vlad was later successful in capturing a prince who was instrumental in the killing of Mircea. Vlad impaled the prince. The Turks captured Vlad himself around 1462 until 1474 (Treptow, 2000). However, while imprisoned he was able to court a member of the royal family and after he was released he married into that family. Also, during his captivity he converted to Catholicism. Moving back to rule again in Romania, he was noted as a cruel and ruthless ruler. Insisting upon honesty and moral behavior, he especially punished women who were found guilty of alleged moral charges (McNally and Florescu, 1994). There were stories of one execution of an unfaithful wife. Her breasts were cut off, then skinned and impaled in the public square with her breasts' skin lying on a table beside her. Women who violated the moral laws of the community were often treated in a similar fashion. Their breasts were cut off, often impaled by red-hot stakes that were forced through the vagina up through the mouth or neck (Florescu, 1989).

So how did Vlad the Impaler move from a ruler of a small community in Romania to Count Dracula? Perhaps because of his extreme cruelty and inhuman-ness, and later the writings of Bram Stoker, he became the model for Dracula.

True Vampires

Vlad, was known for his cruelty and his punishments he meted out to those who fell as victims to his reign. As a defender of Wallachia against the Ottoman Empire in Romania, he had his favorite method of punishment for his conquered enemies. He would execute his victims by impalement. He would have a person dropped onto a sharpened pole starting from between the legs. The weight of the person would force the tip of the torso through the chest cavity of the neck or through the mouth or chest.

Countess Elizabeth Bathory (1560–1614) was a Hungarian countess from a prominent family. Afraid of the aging process, one day she accidently spilled a small amount of blood from one of her handmaidens and became convinced that it had healed the abrasion on her skin and made her skin look younger (Codrescu, 1995). Because of the renowned family and the riches, she was able to secure a large number of maidens from the nearby village in Slovakia. She developed a plan to drain the blood of almost six hundred young women in order to bathe in their blood in an attempt to slow the aging process (Penrose, 1970). The local authori-ties arrested her but the religious leaders convinced the local judges not to charge Bathory. However, four of her female servants were charged and put to death, one by beheading, and the others being thrown on a fire. She died of natural causes in her prison cell at the age of 54 (McNally, 1983).

But the history of vampires goes further back than the 17th century. In ancient Hebrew literature, Lilith was thought to be Adam's first wife (Isaiah 34:14). A strong-willed woman who would not be subservient to Adam, she refused a sexual position under Adam. Depending on who is telling the story, one insists that Lilith left Adam of her own volition and moved to the Red Sea area where she was found sexually cavorting with demons. Others tell that God raised her to Heaven where she became the wife of Lucifer (Isaiah 34:14).

In ancient Greece, Lamia was a vampire who conceived a child by Zeus. When Hera, the wife of Zeus, discovered this, she forced Lamia to eat her own child that caused her own physical disfigurement. She became a demon over the ages that stole children and drained men of their blood after sex (Columbia Electronic Encyclopedia, 2007).

Arnold Paole, a Serbian soldier who lived in the early 1700s, related a story that he witnessed a vampire attack and was bitten. He said that at a later date a vampire attacked him. A folktale at the time stated that if you were a victim of a vampire, one way to fend off the effects was to eat some of the dirt at the gravesite of the vampire. He did so, he said. Paole died in the late 1720s, and people feared him even after he was dead, convinced he was a vampire. A score of villagers stated that Paole appeared to them as they slept in their beds. He would crawl upon them in bed and suffocate them simply by lying upon them. Four people in the village died within a month. After their deaths, the villagers dug up Paole's body and found it in a "vampire condition." They then dug up sixteen "victims" of Paole and found them all in the same condition as Paole. Four of these "vampires" were infants. This was all done within two months of their deaths. The knowledge of decomposition was not as sophisticated as it is today; decomposition to skeletal remains can take several months and in some cases even years. One villager remarked that when he stabbed Paole, the corpse emitted a groan and oozed a large amount of blood, not an unusual case in today's world of forensic science knowledge (Vargas, 2008).

Peter Plogojowitz, a Serbian peasant, was another vampire of the same era. After his death in 1739, nine fellow villagers died within a 24-hour period. Before the villagers passed away, they all told the same story. Plogojowitz appeared to them in their bed and tried to strangle them or choked them to death. This occurred until ten weeks after his Plogojowitz's (Bunson, 1993).

Peter Kurten, a German serial killer and vampire, was dubbed the Vampire of Dusseldorf, by the media. He killed a series of children and adults principally in 1929 in Dusseldorf. At his trial for nine murders and seven attempted murders, he confessed that the sight of blood excited him, and he also drank some of the victim's blood. He also confessed to 79 offenses including the murders and attempted murders. Kurten was executed on July 2, 1931 by the guillotine (Holmes and Holmes, 2009).

In the small town of Paducah in western Kentucky, a small clan of teenage vampires following the instructions of their leader—self-proclaimed vampire, Rod Ferrell—traveled to Florida (see Figure 5.1). Along with other teenagers, Ferrell killed the parents of his girlfriend. He was then apprehended by the local police. For this offense of a double homicide he received the death penalty. However, the courts later ruled that no one under the age of 18 could be executed. His sentence was commuted to life in prison, which he is currently serving. Why were they called vampire killers? Simply put, they drank the blood of themselves, of each other, and also of their victims.

Figure 5.1   Rod Ferrell. (Courtesy of Florida Department of Corrections.)

Cannibalism

Another form of anthropopaghy is cannibalism, eating human flesh. There may be several reasons for the practice of cannibalism. One reason, perhaps, is that a particular society may have sanctioned this type of human behavior. In the late Middle Ages, people in Europe purchased ground up mummy remains as a form of medicine. History has informed us of several American Indian tribes that have practiced cannibalism: Mohawk, Utes, Chippewa, and others. The famous Donner Party in the western United States in the mid-1850s was a case of a group of people eating their comrades to survive.

Fritz Haarman was a serial killer in Hanover, Germany. From 1919 to 1924 he allegedly killed as least 24 people, mostly young males. He would kill most of his victims by biting through their necks. He ate their flesh and drank their blood along with his companion, Hans Gran. Haarman was executed for his crimes (Holmes, 1983; Lessing, 1992).

There are many stories of serial killers who were also cannibals. Perhaps one of the most famous was Jeffrey Dahmer (1994). In 1992 Dahmer was found guilty of 17 murders of young men in Milwaukee. When the police went into his apartment, they found a skull, fingers, and other body parts. However, there was only one certified case in which he ate parts, an arm muscle, of a human body. Dahmer, it seems, was more interested in making his victims pseudomummies by drilling a hole into their skulls and into the brains. He wanted to make them his sex slaves (J. Dahmer, interview). Another inmate beat Dahmer to death in prison in 1994 (Mann and Williamson, 2006).

Edmund Kemper is another serial killer who allegedly ate some of his victims' body parts. Kemper was sent to live with his grandparents when he was 15. One day he killed his grandmother, Maude, on August 27, 1964, and later when he grandfather, Ed Emil, walked into the kitchen he killed him too. Kemper was 15 at the time. He called his mother, confessed to her his crime, and she called the police. Kemper was sent to prison and released when he turned 21. Kemper proceeded on a killing spree of murder, killing the following young women:

- Mary Anne Pisce, May 5, 1972
- Anita Luchese, May 5, 1972
- Aiko Koo, September 14, 1972
- Cindy Schall, January 8, 1973
- Rosalind Thorpe, February 5, 1973
- Alice Lui, February 5, 1973
- Clarnell Strandberg, April 21, 1973
- Sally Hallett, April 21, 1973

After the last murder, Kemper killed his mother and his mother's friend. He decapitated his mother and threw her voice box down the garbage disposal. Kemper drove to Colorado where he called the police and confessed to his crimes. Kemper is presently in prison in California (Cheney, 1976).

Ed Gein was another cannibal as well as a grave robber. Committing his crimes of murder and grave robberies around 1957, he died of natural causes in prison in 1984 (Schechter, 1998a). Albert Fish was another serial killer and a cannibal. When apprehended by the police in New York State, on his stove was a stew that he had made from the body parts of his last victim, 12-year-old Grace Budd. Fish was executed for his crimes (Schechter, 1998b).

Usually when one thinks of Ted Bundy, we do not think of a cannibal. But Bundy did bite off the right nipple of one of his victims and ingested it. He also bit the buttocks of several other victims and ingested those chunks of flesh. When Ronald Holmes talked with Bundy on death row in Florida concerning his murder of Lisa Levy and the attacks inside the Chi Omega House in 1978, he said that he had not killed in more than two years, and he was in such a frenzy in December 1987, he attacked without thinking or too much planning, and he killed without a rational and deliberate plan. His attack on the bodies of those victims included cannibalism but not vampirism. But had it not been for those bite marks on the bodies of his victims, and the identification of the teeth marks by a forensic odontologist, Bundy might have been found not guilty in that case (Rule, 2008).

But what impels one to drink someone's blood or eat another's flesh. In spiritual terms, in some religions, one drinks the wine that has been changed into the blood of Christ and the bread that has also been changed into the body of Christ. In that way, the communicant receives the qualities of God by eating the flesh and drinking the blood. This is spiritual anthropopaghy. But there are those who drink human blood and eat human flesh because they receive a personal and sexual gratification from the act. In talking with Bundy (interview, March, 1985) on death row, I (RMH) asked him about his ingesting the right nipple of one of his victim and the buttocks of another victim. He said, almost apologetically, that he bit and swallowed a small part of the buttocks of a 16-year-old victim on an impulse, a sexual fantasy he had for a long time. He said he first thought about it when he was 11 or 12 years of age. He read some stories of vampires and cannibals in true detective magazines and thought it would something he might like to do. He added that when he was in the Chi Omega House killing one co-ed, he thought of it again and decided to bite off her nipple. He also said that it was just as he had imagined it to be.

Self-Cannibalism

There is a certain amount of self-cannibalism that occurs among all of us. The body may consume dead cells from the tongue and cheeks. Also ingesting one's blood from a small cut on a finger should not be considered anthropopaghy or autovampirism. But there are some people who will eat parts of their own body of their own volition as a form of body mutilation. There are others who are forced to eat their own body parts by some with power over them. Elizabeth Bathory forced some of her female servants to eat parts of their own body. Thomas Harris (2001), in one of his books *Hannibal*, forced a character to eat his own nose and there were other acts of cannibalism in that book. There are many examples of autocannibalism and autovampirism. What does one hope to gain from this form of human behavior? Is it ultimate power in the case of Elizabeth Bathory or in the fictional character of Hannibal Lecter? Is it an attempt to gain the good qualities of the person of whom we are partaking? Or is it a psychological abnormality that manifests itself as in the cases of Bundy, Gein, or Fish? In a report by Roach (2003), he suggests that humans carry a gene that has evolved over the years as protection against brain diseases that can be spread by eating human flesh. Does a sense of compulsion accompany the possession of that gene? Was it that gene that caused Bundy, Gein, or Fish to do what they did? These questions need further scientific investigations.

Vampires have traditionally been thought of as only bloodsucking creatures, but there may also be "psychic" vampires who feed off the emotions of others. But when the ordinary person thinks of a vampire it is one who has fangs, floats into a room, emerges from a bat form, and slowly come to its victim with a snarl and mouth open, its fangs ready to bite into the neck of its confused and vulnerable victim. But there are other traits:

- *Immortality* is a belief that vampires live forever or at least possessing a very long life span.
- The vampire also has great *strength*, at least stronger than the average man.
- The vampire also has *great speed and agility.* The vampire is able to move about a room in eye-blinking speed.
- The vampire appears to have *psychic abilities* from reading their victim's mind to control.

- *Rapid healing* is another asset of the vampire. The vampire cannot be healed by abnormal means and if wounded the wound can be seen healing itself.
- *Invisibility* is another trait. Many believe that the vampire can be invisible if it chooses so.
- *Extraordinary senses* are attributes of the vampire. In this instance, the vampire can detect the smallest changes in an environment such a temperature, lightness or darkness, movements of even tiny insects. The vampire can hear sounds undetectable to normal human hearing.

In Boston, a headmaster wrote to parents at home attempting to quash rumors that there was a vampire at the school. Law enforcement officers stated that two young female students bullied another female student who liked to dress in "Gothic-style" clothing. The students started spreading a rumor that the third girl was a vampire and had cut someone's neck and sucked her blood. The students stated that two or three other girls always carry an umbrella to shade themselves from the sun, proving that they are vampires.

Another student reported to a local newspaper that another male student was rumored to be a werewolf and had threatened to bring a gun to school because he was through being bullied.

Source: **Woolhouse and Cramer, *Boston Globe*, March 27, 2009.**

Of course, not everyone agrees there are true vampires, bloodsucking creatures who overcome death by sucking and then drinking human blood. We think of a vampire as someone who is dead, but rises from the dead out of a coffin at night to seek victims to drink their blood. There are few people at this extreme other than in the movies people. But stories still abound.

Vampire and Cannibal Organizations

There is a national organization for cannibals headquartered in Phoenix, Arizona. It is called The Phoenix. Founded in 2002, the members are vampires, cannibals, and donors of flesh and blood. The organizers are quick to add that they are not a dating service, but admit it is a good place to learn the techniques for their activities.

Armin Meiwes is listed as an inspiration for cannibals worldwide. Meiwes, a German, advertised on the Internet, "looking for a well-built 18–30-year-old to be slaughtered and then consumed" ("German cannibal," 2003). One man personally met with Meiwes, Bernd Jurgen Brandes, on Christmas Day 2001. They went to Meiwes's house, which he shared with his overbearing and domineering mother. After making a two-hour video of their homosexual lovemaking, and plying Brandes with alcohol and sleeping pills, Meiwes crudely cut off the penis of Brandes. Both rushed to the kitchen where they tried to cook it on the stove. For whatever reason, both agreed that it was too "chewy" and not what they expected. They went back to the "slaughter room" that Meiwes had built for this sole purpose. Finally to expedite his death, Brandes was stabbed in the chest and his throat was slashed until he was dead. Brandes was hanged from the wall on meat hooks, skinned, and Meiwes tried to grind his bones into flour. In January 2004, Miewes was tried and convicted of manslaughter and sentenced to eight and half years in prison. In Frankfurt, Germany, two years later, the court convicted him of murder at his retrial, and he was sentenced to life imprisonment. A true, live Hannibal Lecter!

The Extent and Danger of Modern Day Vampires and Cannibals

It is not our belief that there will be hordes of anthropopagists on the loose in our cities or towns. But history tells us there will be isolated cases that arise with some regularity across the nation where innocent victims are predated upon. There will be Jeffrey Dahmers, Ted Bundys, and Richard Carpenters who murder scores of people, but people lose sight of their "content of action." There will be young people who experiment with drinking blood, not satisfied with their own or with volunteers. They will seek out animals to satisfy their perceived need to eat raw flesh and drink warm blood.

Yes, there will not be hordes of Draculas; but one Rod Ferrell is too many. The eating of human flesh and drinking of blood even with the circumstances of the Donner Party is one that will disgust and repel many. The popularity of the vampires and cannibals in movies and on TV may influence some to try the deeds but not turn otherwise "normal" young people into these kinds of predators. They have other defects in their psyche that result in their acts of fatal predation.

Thus, the acts of Bela Lugosi, Vincent Price, Christopher Lee, and Hannibal Lecter must be seen for what they are, not as true stories that put each of us in a focus in mortal danger but out of the minds of otherwise normal writers and actors.

Discussion Questions

1. Why do you believe vampire movies are so popular?
2. Which horror movie is your favorite? Why do you think that is?
3. Are you aware of any modern vampires? Did you look up the case of the vampires from Kentucky who killed in Florida?

4. Look up the home site of the Cannibal Café. What is your reaction? Share your thoughts with others.
5. Prepare a report on the Phoenix Vampires/Vampyres/Donors/Swans. What are the goals and objectives of this organization? Discuss your findings with the class.

References

Barber, P. (1988). *Vampires: Burial and death; Folklore and reality.* New York: Yale University Press.

Bunson, M. (1993). *The vampire encyclopedia.* London: Thames and Hudson.

Cheney, M. (1976). *The co-ed killer.* New York: Walker and Co.

Columbia Electronic Encyclopedia. 2007. New York: Columbia University Press.

Codrescu, A. (1995). *Blood countess.* New York: Simon & Schuster.

Dahmer, L. (1994). *A father's story.* New York: William Morrow & Co.

Dundes, A. (1998). *The vampire: A casebook.* Madison, WI: University of Wisconsin Press.

Florescu, R. (1989). *Dracula of many faces.* New York: Little Brown and Co.

Frost, B. (1989). *The monster with a thousand faces.* Madison, WI: University of Wisconsin Press.

German cannibal tells of fantasy. (2003). *BBC News,* December 3. http://news.bbc.uk/2/hi/europe/3286721.stm (accessed November 17, 2008).

Harris, T. (2001). *Hannibal.* New York: Random House.

Holmes, R. (1983). *The sex offender and the criminal justice system.* Springfield, IL: Thomas Publishing Co.

Holmes, R., and Holmes, S. (2009). *Sex crimes.* Thousand Oaks, CA: Sage.

Kittredge, G. L. (1929). *Witchcraft in Old and New England.* Cambridge, MA: Harvard University Press.

Lessing, T. (1992). *Monsters of the Weimar.* Flanders: Nemesis Publications.

Linder, D. (2005). *A brief history of witchcraft persecutions before Salem.* Kansas City: University of Missouri Press.

Mann, R., and Williamson, M. (2006). *Forensic detective—How I cracked the world's toughest cases.* New York: Ballentine Books.

McNally, R. (1983). *Dracula was a woman: In search of the Blood Countess of Transylvania.* New York: McGraw-Hill.

McNally, R., and Florescu, R. (1994). *In search of Dracula,* rev. ed. New York: Houghton Mifflin.

Penrose, V. (1970). *Bloody countess.* London: Calder and Boyers.

Roach, J. (2003). Cannibalism: Normal for early humans? *National Geographic,* April 10.

Rule, A. (2008). *The stranger beside me.* New York: Pocket Books.

Schechter, H. (1998a). *Deviant: The shocking true story of Ed Gein, the original psycho.* New York: Pocket Books.

Schechter, H. (1998b). *Deranged: The shocking true story of America's most fiendish killer.* New York: Pocket Books.

Stoker, B. (1897). *Dracula.* New York: Barnes & Noble Classics, 2005.

Summers, M. (1980). *The vampire in Europe.* London: The Aquarian Press.

Treptow, K. (2000). *Vlad III Dracula: The life and times of the historical Dracula*. Portland, OR: Center for Romania Studies.

Vargas, F. (2008). *A dubious place*. Paris: Viviane Hamy.

Woolhouse, M., and Cramer, M. (2009). Vampire rumors spur alert at Boston Latin on bullying. *Boston Globe*, March 27.

Suggested Reading

Friesen, J. (2008). "Please kill me" accused begs in court. *The Globe and Mail*, August 1. http://theglobeandmail.com/servlet/story/LAC.20080802.Death01/TPstory/ (National) (accessed November 24, 2008).

Miller, E. (2002). *Dracula: Sense and nonsense*. Greeley, CO: Desert Island Press.

Summers, M. (2005). *Vampires and vampirism*. Mineola, NY: Dover Press.

Twitchell, J. (1981). *The living dead: A study of the vampire in Romantic literature*. Durham, NC: Duke University Press.

Wolf, L. (1972). *A dream of Dracula*. New York: Popular Library.

Wright, D. (1973). *The book of vampires*. New York: Causeway Books.

Chapter 6

Mass Murder

Introduction

In December 2008, a man dressed as Santa Claus knocked at the door of a family celebrating Christmas with friends and relatives. An 8-year-old girl opened the door and was shot in the face. The man opened fire on the other members of the gathering. He then set the home afire. Moving on to his brother's house, he set a second house afire, and then shot himself. What was the motivation for these scenes of mass murder? Apparently there was some type of discord between him and his estranged wife of his one child.

What is mass murder? Mass murder is the killing of three or more people at one time and one place. It is different from serial murder, which was defined in Chapter 4. It is also different from spree murder, which is the killing of three or more people in less than a 30-day period with a significant cooling off period between the murders and also usually accompanied by the commission of another felony such as robbery (Holmes and Holmes, 2001a).

History of Mass Murder in the United States

America's consciousness to the social problem of mass murder was awakened on July 31, 1966, when Charles Whitman picked up his wife from her job in downtown Austin, Texas. Shortly after noon, he dropped his wife off at their apartment and then drove to his mother's home. He had previously written two notes: one note was devoted to the details of how he was going to kill his mother and the second was how he was going to kill other innocent people. He drove to his mother's house and stabbed her five times. He left the following note on a nightstand next to her bed (Statesman.com):

To whom it may concern,

I have just taken my mother's life. I am very upset over having done it. However, I feel that if there is a heaven, she is definitely there now. And if there is no life after, I have relieved her of her suffering here on earth. The intense hatred I feel for my father is beyond description. My mother gave that man the best 25 years of her life and because she finally took enough of his beatings, humiliation and degradation and tribulations that I am sure no one but she and he will ever know—to leave him. He has chosen to treat her like a slut that you would bed down with, accept her favors and then throw a pitance in return.

I am truly sorry that this is the only way I could see to relieve her sufferings but I think it is the best.

Let there be no doubt in your mind I loved that woman with all my heart.

If there exists a God, let him understand my actions and judge me accordingly.

Charles J. Whitman

After Whitman killed his mother, he drove home. He then fatally stabbed his wife four times while she was asleep. He then typed another note (Statesman. com):

I don't quite understand what it is that compels me to type this letter. Perhaps it is to leave some vague reason for the actions I have recently performed. I don't really understand myself these days. I am supposed to be an average reasonable and intelligent young man. However, lately (I don't recall when it started) I have been a victim of many unusual and irrational thoughts. These thoughts constantly recur, and it requires a tremendous mental effort to concentrate on useful and progressive tasks. In March when my parents made a physical break I noticed a great deal of stress. I consulted a Dr. Cochrum at the University Health Center and asked him to recommend someone that I could consult with about some psychiatric disorders I felt I had ...

Charles J. Whitman

On the next day, Whitman climbed to the top of the Texas Tower at the University of Texas and shot at people for the next two hours. After shooting 32 people and killing 14 more (see Table 6.1; Lavergne, 1997), people wondered about what would cause this ex-Marine to do such a thing. An autopsy was done. A brain tumor was found. It was, however, never fully determined if this was the cause of this incident of mass murder. But what has been learned was that Whitman was 25 years old at the time of the shooting, married, a son of divorced parents. He

Table 6.1   Victims of Charles Whitman

Killed
Margaret Whitman, killed in her apartment
Kathy Whitman, killed while she slept
Edna Townsley, receptionist
Marguerite Lamport, killed by shotgun
Mark Gabour, killed by shotgun on stairs
Thomas Eckman, shoulder wound
Robert Boyer, back wound, visiting physics professor
Thomas Ashton, chest wound, Peace Corps trainee
Thomas Karr, spine wound
Billy Speed, police officer, shoulder/chest wound
Harry Walchuk, doctoral student and father of six
Paul Sonntag, shot through the mouth, age 18
Claudia Rutt, age 18
Karen Griffith, chest wound
Unborn child, fatally injured when Claire Wilson was shot in her abdomen
Roy Schmidt, electrician, shot outside his truck
David Gunby, survived the initial shooting but required life-long dialysis as a result of his injuries. More than 30 years after the shooting, he announced he was quitting dialysis and died within a week
Wounded
John Scott Allen
Billy Bedford
Roland Ehlke
Ellen Evgenides
Avelino Esparza

(continued)

Table 6.1 Victims of Charles Whitman (Continued)

F. L. Foster
Robert Frede
Mary Frances Gabour
Michael Gabour
Irma Garcia
Nancy Harvey
Robert Heard
Alex Hernandez
Morris Hohmann
Devereau Huffman
Homar J. Kelley
Abdul Khashab
Brenda Gail Littlefield
Adrian Littlefield
Dello Martinez
Marina Martinez
David Mattson
Delores Ortega
Janet Paulos
Lana Phillips
Oscar Rovela
Billy Snowden
C. A. Stewart
Carla Sue Wheeler
Claire Wilson
Sandra Wilson

Source: Levin, J., and Fox, J. A. (1985). *Mass murder: America's growing menace.* New York: Plenum Press. (With permission.)

apparently had a deep hatred of his father; believed his father was abusive toward his mother and Whitman himself. When his parents separated at the time of their impending divorce, Whitman became abusive in his behavior, and his distraught parents sought psychiatric counseling for their son. Regardless Whitman himself never was able to fully explain his behavior and his willingness and interest in killing. Be it a result from his brain tumor, his relationship with his father (which does not explain his decision to kill his mother who he said he loved a great deal), or a strange and complex combination of medical and social elements, it will remain a mystery (Lavergne, 1997; Levin and Fox, 1985).

Sometimes we believe there is too much effort being placed on the perpetrators of the crime and too little time spent on the victims of the crimes. We remember the names of mass killers—Elizabeth Bathory, Charles Whitman, Joseph Wesbecker—but know not one name of the many victims they have killed or maimed. This is also true of the serial killers. We know Ted Bundy, Richard Ramirez, and others of this same ilk, but cannot recall one victim. In one way, this tells us of the way we hold the names of the killers in infamy while not only ignoring the dead victims but also the families, friends, and relatives of those who died at the hands of the killers.

Types of Mass Killers

There are two elements in the basic definition of mass murder (Holmes and Holmes, 2001a). One element states that the murder must take place at one time in one place. We can list case after case where this is true. Joseph Wesbecker went to his former place of employment and killed seven former coworkers and then shot himself. In another case, James Oliver Huberty walked out of his home and went to the local McDonald's. He killed 21 customers and wounded 19 others. A police sniper in a building across the street killed Huberty (Gresko, 2004). Dr. Jeffrey MacDonald was convicted of stabbing his two children and his wife. In the first two cases, the victims were former coworkers. In the latter case, the victims were family members. But they were all killed in one place at one time. But suppose there is a case of mass murder when the person goes from one place where he killed two and then went to another location. Would this still be a case of mass murder? From our perspective it is still mass murder. The action was a continual act despite the different locations (McGinnis, 1984).

Classification of Mass Murderers

There is a great attraction to place human behavior into categories. These categories are defined by behavioral dynamics, motivations, victim traits and characteristics, methodologies, motivations, and anticipated rewards (Holmes and Holmes, 1988).

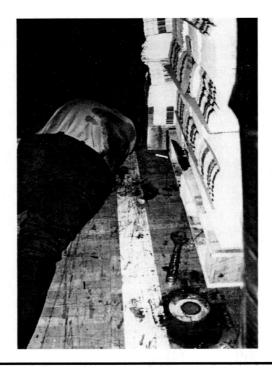

Figure 6.1 A murder victim of Joseph Wesbecker.

In the following, we will discuss the various elements as they apply to mass murderers. While we will not trace the history of mass murderers and mass killers in other countries, we can say that mass murderers have been with us for many years, and it appears that statistics have been kept within only the last 150 years or so. In looking at various sources, it appears also true that there are mass killers present in almost every country (see Table 6.2 for information regarding mass killers in foreign countries).

It would appear that mass killers are more prevalent in the United States. The names of James Oliver Huberty, Charles Whitman, Joseph Wesbecker, Colin Ferguson, and many others are unknown or unreported to the national media. Richard Speck is another famous mass killer. Speck was born in Kirkwood, Illinois, the seventh of eight children to Benjamin Speck and Mary Gladys Sterner. Raised in a religious family, his father died when he was 5, and sometime afterward, his mother took Richard and his younger sister Carolyn to Dallas, Texas. They moved to a section called East Dallas. After the move, his mother married Carl Lindberg, from whom Speck suffered from his drunkenness, abuse, and absences from the home (Chua-Eoan, 2008). Speck was a poor student. By the age of 12, he had begun drinking alcohol, a habit that would last for the rest of his life. He used alcohol partly to ease the pain of headaches he had begun to suffer at the age of 5,

Table 6.2   Alleged and Suspected Mass Murderers in Foreign Countries in the 21st Century

Name	Year	Country	Number Killed
Richard Durn	2002	France	8 killed, 19 wounded
Yan Jianzhong	2002	China	9 killed, 1 wounded
Sergey Semidovskiy	2002	Russia	5 killed 10 wounded
Jamshid Soleimani	2002	Iran	6 killed, 5 wounded
Mohsin Al-Hilali	2003	Yemen	9 killed, 1 wounded
Amugae Cheon	2004	South Korea	6 killed, 4 wounded
Jeong Sang-jin	2004	South Korea	5 killed, 7 wounded
Jian Xueliang	2004	China	Killed 8
Angelo Socco	2005	Italy	3 killed, 9 wounded
Basudev Thapa	2005	Nepal	11 killed, 19 wounded
Weenus Chumkammed	2008	Yemen	8 killed, 1 wounded
Abdullahal-Kohali	2008	Yemen	10 killed, 15 wounded
Jia Yang	2008	China	6 killed, 4 wounded
Jinfu Zhang	2008	China	6 killed, 1 wounded
Nicholas Mucunguzi	2009	Uganda	7 Killed, 6 wounded

after suffering head injuries from a claw hammer with which he'd been playing. He fell out of a tree twice, and at 15 he ran headfirst into a steel girder. Speck dropped out of school in the ninth grade.

Speck, then 24, a drifter born in Illinois, raised in Texas, wandering from petty crime to petty crime and bar to bar. At the age of 19, he had the words "Born to Raise Hell" tattooed on his arm. In Chicago on the night of July 14, 1966, Speck broke into a women's dormitory that housed eight nurses who worked at the South Chicago Community Hospital. With a gun and a butcher's knife, bound and gagged all the residents. Then one by one, he kills them cruelly and with great brutality. His victims were all eulogized as saints, people who had committed their lives to helping others. One of his intended targets, Corazon Amurao, who survived the attack by hiding under a bed, identified Speck. Speck knew there were eight women in the dorm; but he was unaware that a friend was also spending the night. A jury found Speck guilty after a mere 49 minutes of deliberation and he was sentenced to the electric chair. In 1972, however, the U.S. Supreme Court declared the death sentence unconstitutional. Resentenced to hundreds of years in prison, Speck died in 1991. No one claimed his body, which was cremated (Breo and Martin, 1993).

Few mass killers kill for sex; most have other purposes. Holmes and Holmes (2001b) list several kinds of mass killers:

- Disciple
- Family annihilator
- Pseudocommando
- Disgruntled employee
- Disgruntled citizen
- Set-and-run
- Psychotic

Disciple

The first type of mass killer is the disciple. The disciple follows the directions of a charismatic leader. We have seen this in the case of the Charles Manson family (Table 6.3). Tex Watson, a devotee of Manson, allegedly followed the directions of Manson in the killings at the Sharon Tate home and also at the LaBianca home. Leslie von Houten, Patricia Krenwinkel, and Susan Adkins were all followers of Manson and followed his directions to do something "witchy" the nights of the two killings.

The anticipated gain for the disciple mass murderers is psychological. They hope to win the appreciation of the leader. Spatial mobility is also limited with this type of mass killer. They will typically be where the leader is. In this case, they were in California because that is where Manson was.

There are other groups that evolve around a leader who possesses outstanding personal qualities. Jim Jones in Guyana is another example. Over nine hundred people lost their lives when he ordered them to drink a cyanide-laced beverage and join him in heaven. In Waco, Texas, David Koresh was responsible for the deaths of over five hundred people in his religious cult where he too, along with Manson and Jones, proclaimed himself to be the reincarnation of Jesus Christ.

Like some other mass murderers, the disciple killer does not seem to have a problem with the world at large. They are only following the directions of their leader. Marshall Applewhite, a leader of a small group of followers in California convinced his followers to poison themselves because in this way the aliens from space could take their bodies to their spaceships and carry them to everlasting happiness.

In 1972, Applewhite met a 44-year-old nurse named Bonnie Nettles with whom he would later form a cult, Heaven's Gate. He met her at a hospital where he was in the process of recovering from a heart attack. He saw her again in a theater and they started courting each other.

In the meantime, Applewhite declared himself to be the reincarnation of Jesus Christ. In 1975, Applewhite and Nettles convinced 20 people to join their group. Applewhite told them there would be an alien appearance by means of a UFO, but

Table 6.3   Alleged and Suspected Members of the Manson Family

Name	Description
Charles Manson	Jesus Christ, the Devil, the leader of the family.
Susan Adkins	Involved in the Tate and LaBianca killings as well as other cases. Also known as Sadie Mae Glutz, Sexy Sadie, and Sharon King.
Bobby Beausoleil	Involved in the Gary Hinman killing; also known as Cupid, Jasper Cherub, Robert Lee Hardy, and Jason Lee Daniels.
Mary Brunner	First female to join the family, may have been involved in the Gary Hinman killing, also known as Mother Mary, Mary Manson, Linda Dee Moser, Och, and Marioche.
James Craig	Pleaded guilty to being an accessory after the fact in two murders.
Lynette Fromme	One of Manson's earliest followers; assumed leadership after Manson was arrested; also known as Squeaky. She is currently in prison for the attempted assassination of President Gerald Ford.
Sandra Goode	A family member; also known as Sandy.
Steven Grogan	Was with the murderers the night of the LaBianca killings; also involved in the Hinman killing, and possibly involved in the attempted murder of a prosecution witness in the trial against Manson. Also known as Clem Tufts.
Gary Hinman	An attorney, befriended by Manson and later allegedly murdered by the family.
Linda Kasabian	Accompanied the killers on the nights of the Tate and LaBianchi murders.
Pat Krenwinkel	Involved in the Tate and LaBianca killings. In prison.
Leslie Van Houten	Involved in the Tate and LaBianca killings. In prison.

Source: Some of the information here is from Bugliso (1975).

the encounter never happened, and they left the group. However, more people joined and soon the group had almost one hundred members. The mansion at Rancho Santa Fe, California, was the eventual site of the group's mass suicide, however the group moved periodically over the years, preferring to reside in California, Colorado, and New Mexico.

Nettles and Applewhite were nicknamed Ti and Do or the UFO Two. Nettles died in 1985 of cancer and Applewhite led Heaven's Gate alone until his suicide in 1997. On March 19, 1997, Marshall Applewhite taped himself speaking of mass suicide and believed "it was the only way to evacuate this Earth. The Heaven's Gate cult was against suicide but members believed they had no choice and had to leave Earth as quickly as possible. After claiming that a spacecraft was trailing the comet Hale-Bopp, Applewhite convinced 38 followers to commit suicide so that their souls could board the craft. Applewhite believed that after their deaths, a UFO would take their souls to another "level of existence above human," which Applewhite described as being both physical and spiritual. Some might consider this comparable to what mainstream Christians envision as heaven. This and other UFO-related beliefs held by the group have led some observers to characterize the group as a type of UFO religion. Applewhite committed suicide with 38 other members in Rancho Santa Fe, California, by mixing phenobarbital with applesauce or pudding, then washing it down with vodka. They also placed plastic bags over their heads after ingesting the mix to ensure asphyxiation in case the drugs did not kill them (Lalich, 2004).

Family Annihilator

The family annihilator (Dietz, 1986) is a very frequent type of mass killer. John List (Figure 6.2) is an example. List, in the early morning hours on December 7, 1972, killed his mother, wife, and three children. His mother was found in a closet on the second floor and the wife and children were found on the floor on the first floor of the large house where the List family resided. The family dog was also found dead in the basement.

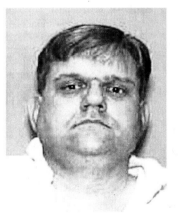

Figure 6.2 John List. (Courtesy of Texas Department of Corrections.)

During the marriage, the List family encountered many financial problems and lived from paycheck to paycheck. The wife was reportedly an alcoholic and John List was reportedly not in love with her. After the murder, List disappeared for seventeen years. He moved from New Jersey to Colorado, married for the second time, and then moved to Virginia. He was now known as Robert Clark. The List case was presented on *America's Most Wanted* TV program. The program was televised and two months later FBI agents arrested John after a neighbor alerted the TV show that List lived in her area. List was placed on trial and was given five consecutive life sentences (Benford and Johnson, 1991; Holmes and Holmes, 2001a, 2001b; Ryzuk, 1990; Sharkey, 1990). List died from complications of pneumonia at age 82 on March 21, 2008, while in prison custody at a Trenton, New Jersey, hospital.

There are other family annihilators. In 1988, Ronald Simmons went on a killing rampage and killed 16 people. Living in Arkansas after his discharge from the U.S. Air Force, Simmons killed a former coworker and his employer. He also killed 14 family members. On May 31, 1988, Arkansas governor (later President) Bill Clinton signed Simmons's execution warrant, and on June 25, 1990, Simmons died by the method he had chosen, lethal injection.

In Channelview, Texas, Coy Wesbrook was invited to his ex-wife's house for a party in November 1997. Wesbrook thought there was a possibility of him and his ex-wife, Gloria, getting back together. At the party, Gloria went to another room where she had sex with two men. Wesbrook went outside to his car and brought back a hunting rifle. He killed his ex-wife and four other people. Wesbrook was convicted and sentenced to death. No date has been set for his execution.

The basic motivation for the family annihilator rests within the mind of the mass murderer. There is no one to tell him to kill, like the disciple mass killer. As far as spatial mobility, the family annihilator is usually a long-term member of the community. He has lived in the area with his family for an extended period of time. And unlike the other mass killers we will speak of, this mass murderer usually kills people he knows.

Pseudocommando

Dietz (1986) describes the pseudocommando mass killer as a mass murderer who has a keen interest in guns and weapons. This kind of mass killer usually stockpiles weapons in his home and will use them in his attacks on others. This person sees himself as an expert in weapons and is willing to exercise his expertise in the extermination of strangers. The victims are strangers to this type of mass murderer. They may simply be in the wrong place at the wrong time, but the consequence is still the same.

Table 6.4 Alleged and Suspected Mass Murderers in the United States in the 21st Century

Name	Year	Location	Victims
Luther Casteel	2001	Illinois	3 killed, 15 wounded
James Llewelyn	2002	New Jersey	6 killed, 1 wounded
Douglas Williams*	2003	Mississippi	6 killed, 8 wounded
Chai Vang	2004	Wisconsin	6 killed, 2 wounded
Terry Ratzmann*	2005	Wisconsin	7 dead, 4 wounded
Kyle Huff	2006	Washington	6 killed, 2 wounded
Jennifer San Marco*	2006	California	7 killed
Robert Hawkins*	2007	Nebraska	8 killed, 4 wounded
Tyler Patterson*	2007	Wisconsin	6 killed, 1 wounded
Nicholas Sheley	2008	Arkansas	8 killed
Michael McLendon*	2009	Alabama	10 killed, 6 wounded
Robert Stewart	2009	North Carolina	8 killed, 3 wounded
Jiverly Wong*	2009	New York	13 dead, 4 wounded

* Committed suicide.

James Oliver Huberty might be considered a good example of the pseudo-commando mass murderer. Despite spending the morning with his family visiting the local zoo, that afternoon as his wife was preparing to take a short nap, he told her that he was leaving. He was going to "hunt humans." Armed with several guns and rifles, and an ample supply of ammunition, Huberty walked only a short way to the local McDonald's restaurant and killed 19 people. When the police further investigated the case, they found huge stacks of weapons and ammunition in Huberty's basement, as well as a homemade firing range constructed in his basement. Huberty was new to San Ysidro, California. He had just moved there with his family after he was terminated from his job in Ohio as a welder. Perhaps he was angry with his employer or simply angry at the world for his present situation. Regardless, his motivation to kill rested inside his own personality. His spatial mobility is limited. He kills in his own area, an area that he is familiar. His victims are strangers.

Table 6.5   Mass Murderers of 20th Century

Mass Murderer	Dates	Victims	Location	Disposition
Larry Gene Ashbrook	1999	7	Fort Worth, TX, USA	Suicide
Jorjik Avanesian	1996	7	Glendale, CA, USA	Life
George Banks	1982	13	Wilkes-Barre, PA, USA	12 death sentences
Mark Barton	1999	12	Atlanta, GA, USA	Suicide
Eric Borel	1995	13	Tasmania, Australia	Suicide
Martin Bryant	1996	35	Pacific Southwest Airline	Condemned
David Burke	1987	43	Vernon, British Columbia	Died in Plane Crash
Mark Chahal	1999	9	Houston, TX, USA	Suicide
Robert Coulson	1992	5	Amityville, NY, USA	Condemned
Ronnie DeFeo	1974	6	Houston, TX, USA	6 life terms
Ray Martin DeFord (11 years old)	1996	8	Portland, Oregon, USA	Ongoing
Humberto De La Torre	1982	25	Portland, Oregon, USA	625 years
Mark Essex	1973	7	Los Angeles, CA, USA	Shot by police
Gunter Hermann Ewen	1999	5	New Orleans, LA, USA	Suicide
Colin Ferguson	1993	6	Germany and France	Life

(continued)

Table 6.5   Mass Murderers of 20th Century (Continued)

Mass Murderer	Dates	Victims	Location	Disposition
Genildo Ferreira de Franca	1997	8	Sao Paulo, Brazil	Suicide
Gian Luigi Ferri	1993	8	San Francisco, CA, USA	Suicide
Wade Frankum	1991	8	Strathfield, Australia	Suicide
Baruch Goldstein	1994	29	Israel	Unknown
Julio Gonzales	1990	87	Bronx, NY, USA	Unknown
Jack Gilbert Graham	1955	44	Denver, CO, USA	Unknown
David Gray	1990	13	New Zealand	Shot by Police
Thomas Hamilton	1996	17	Dunblane, Scotland	Suicide
Eric Harris & Dylan Klebold	1999	13	Littleton, CO, USA	Both suicide
George Jo Hennard	1991	23	Bell County, TX, USA	Suicide
James Oliver Huberty	1984	21	San Ysidro, CA, USA	Shot by Sniper
Mitchell Johnson & Andrew Golden	1998	5	Jonesboro, AR, USA	5 & 7 years (juveniles)
Andrew Kehoe	1927	45	Bath, Michigan, USA	Suicide
Marc Lepine	1989	15	Montreal, Quebec, Canada	Suicide
Daniel Patric Lyman	1987	7	Tacoma, WA, USA	Suicide
Timothy McVeigh	1995	168	Oklahoma City, OK, USA	Executed
James Edward Pough	1990	10	Jacksonville, FL, USA	Suicide

Table 6.5   Mass Murderers of 20th Century (Continued)

Mass Murderer	Dates	Victims	Location	Disposition
Anton Probst	1866	8+	Philadelphia, PA, USA	Hanged
Saeed Qashash	1999	12	Jordan, Israel	Hanged
Larry Keith Robison	1982	5	Texas, USA	Executed
James Ruppert	1975	11	Hamilton, Ohio, USA	Institutionalized
Michael Ryan	1987	16	Hungerford, England	Suicide
Pat Sherrill	1986	14	Edmond, Oklahoma, USA	Suicide
Roland Smith	1995	7	New York City, NY, USA	Suicide
Richard Speck	1966	8+	Chicago, IL, USA	400 years
Mark Storm	1997	5	Wheeling, WV, USA	Suicide
Howard Unruh	1949	13	East Camden, NJ, USA	Institutionalized
Joseph Wesbecker	1989	7	Kentucky, USA	Suicide
Charles Whitman	1966	18	University of Texas, USA	Shot by Police
Coy Wayne Wesbrook	1997	5	Dallas, Texas	Condemned

Disgruntled Employee

Disgruntled employee killers are often former employees of the company where they commit their act of mass murder. On July 7, 2003, a Lockheed Martin plant employee left a meeting in the plant and went to his car. The employee, Douglas Williams, returned and opened fire, killing six people. The employees stated that Williams, who is white, stated that he was going to kill blacks and threatened many of the black employees of the plant for a long period of time. He killed nine people.

The worst post office massacre took place on August 20, 1986, in Edmond, Oklahoma. Patrick "Sandy" Sherrill, a 44-year-old part-time postal worker attached to the main post office in this suburb of Oklahoma County, had been warned the day before his killing spree that he was facing a dismissal for unsatisfactory work. It was not the first time Sherrill had been in trouble, and reports from the postal authorities claimed that he had already been under suspension once in the year since he joined as a postman in 1985.

Sherrill was always prepared to tell anybody that with an inclination to listen that he was a Vietnam veteran, which was quite untrue. However, he was a member of the Oklahoma National Guard, and a considerable marksman with their competition team. In this position of trust, Sherrill was able to withdraw guns from the ONG arsenal for the purpose of entering shooting competitions, and on April 5, 1986, he borrowed a .45-caliber automatic pistol. On August 10, 1986, he borrowed an identical weapon and three hundred rounds of ammunition.

On the hot Wednesday morning of August 20, 1986, wearing his regulation postman's uniform, he drove to work as usual, taking with him the two .45s plus his own .22-caliber handgun and the ammunition. He walked toward the post office, stopping just once to shoot dead a fellow worker who was crossing the parking lot, before passing through the employees' entrance into the single story building. After locking several doors in order to maximize his kill, Sherrill began, in the words of the police, "shooting people as though they were sitting ducks." Although FBI marksmen were deployed around the building after an employee escaped and raised the alarm, Sherrill refused to speak to the specially trained siege negotiators.

When the police eventually stormed the building they found the bodies of fourteen men and women, and seven other badly wounded victims. Sherrill lay dead where he had put a single bullet through his own head, his arsenal of guns and ammunition beside him (Robbins, 1986).

The disgruntled employee killer is often geographically stable. He has been an employee of a company for an extended period of time. He normally knows the people he kills. Joseph Wesbecker had been an employee of Standard Gravure for more than twenty years. On September 14, 1989, he went in the plant to look for certain people—black people. Wesbecker killed seven people, wounded twelve others, and then killed himself. The killer, twice divorced and the father of two grown sons, had been in a mental hospital at least two times in the past couple years (Smothers, 1989).

Thus the motivation to kill rests within the personality of the killer. He has defined certain people or groups of people as unworthy to live. He has taken on the responsibility to "get rid" of the bad people at work.

Disgruntled Citizen

The disgruntled citizen commits mass murder because he is upset with others whom he believes have wronged him in some fashion. William Cruse, an elderly white male, decided to kill. He entered a shopping center mall in Hollywood, Florida, and killed six innocent shoppers. Cruse was convinced that his neighbors in Palm Bay, Florida, gossiped about him, spreading the rumor that he was a homosexual. A retired librarian, Cruse was 59 years old when he went on an all-night shooting spree. Around 6 p.m. on April 23, 1987, two boys decided to taunt Cruse by continually walking back and forth past his house shouting obscenities. The librarian grabbed his guns and a bag of ammunition and headed out after the boys. When he fired at them, he missed, instead hitting an innocent 14-year-old bystander who was playing basketball in his driveway. Frustrated, Cruse jumped into his truck and drove to the local Publix supermarket. Once there, he opened fire in the parking lot, killing 2 students instantly. A stray bullet wounded a woman as she sat in her car. Hearing her cries for help, Cruse walked over and shot her in the head to finish the job. After failing to get into Publix, he drove across the street to Winn-Dixie Supermarket where two policemen met him. The first policeman was mortally wounded when Cruse opened fired on his patrol car. The second policeman emptied his revolver at Cruse without ever hitting him. In return, he nearly severed the lawman's leg with one shot, then walked over and shot him in the head as he tried frantically to reload. Once inside the Winn-Dixie, he executed one customer as he tried to flee and secured himself a hostage. After a six-hour standoff, he finally surrendered, releasing the hostage unharmed. In all, the death count stood at six, with ten people wounded. At trial he pleaded not guilty by reason of insanity and several psychiatrists testified that he was a paranoid schizophrenic. The jury, however, did not agree and he was sentenced to death. Cruse was 82 when he died of natural causes on November 29, 2009.

PENNSYLVANIA MAN KILLS 3, HIMSELF, WOUNDS 9

On August 4, 2009, George Sodini walked in the LA Fitness center in Bridgeville, Pa. According to his diary, he had planned this mass killing for several months. One line stated, "Women just don't like me. There are 30 million women in the US (my estimate) and I cannot find one." He complained of not having a girlfriend since 1984, not having a date since May 2008, and not having sex for 19 years.

His three victims were Heidi Overmier, 46; Elizabeth Gannon, 49; and Jody Billingsley, 38.

Source: Armas, G., *Courier Journal*, August 4, 2009, A-8.

In another case in Florida, Carl Brown was annoyed at the employees of an auto mechanic shop who had done some work on his car. He killed eight employees of the shop. As he fled, he rode his bicycle toward his home. Several witnesses overtook him and shot him. They ran over him in a car making certain he was dead.

The motivation to kill for the disgruntled citizen is intrinsic to the killer (Holmes and Holmes, 2001a). The killer perceives that society has wronged him and he will "teach" society a lesson. The anticipated gain is psychological. There is no personal gain here, no money, no insurance, nothing of this sort. The killer murders people who usually have little if anything to do with his personal situation. The killer believes that society will now pay attention to his problems and sympathize with him. This type of killer is also geographically stable; he has been in the area for some time and considers the area his home community.

Set-and-Run

The set-and-run mass murderer is different from the others discussed thus far. He is apart from the scene by the time the criminal justice professionals have arrived. His weapon is often poisons, bombs, explosives, and other timing devices that are set to go off after he has left the scene. The set-and-run killer has no desire to commit suicide or to force the police to kill him. This type of killer may also be a paid killer; if this is true, then the motivation to kill rests outside his personality. If he is killing because he believes something or someone has wronged him, then the motivation lies within the personality. The anticipated gain is psychological. Perhaps this type of mass killer is best termed a set-and-run killer for hire (Holmes and Holmes, 2001b).

The Tylenol Killer in the early 1980s in Chicago was perhaps a set-and-run mass killer. Seven people were killed by medications that they purchased at different drug stores in different neighborhoods. The unknown killer had apparently stolen or purchased packages of capsules over a period of time, then replaced the capsules of medications with cyanide. His motivation to kill is unknown since the killer has never been caught, but if we were to develop a psychological profile of this killer, the elements would include:

- the killer is a white male
- at the time of the killings, he was in his twenties
- he lived in an area of the various drug stores
- he was single
- he was a shoplifter with a minor police record
- he was a drug user
- he has limited education, some college, but no degree
- he has few friends and a social loner
- he drives a small foreign made automobile
- he works at a menial-type, low paying job

There are other types of products that have been used in this manner but these have been in other cities and are not thought to have been the work of the Tylenol Killer.

The Tylenol Killer had no relationship with his victims. They are complete strangers who just happened to buy the product. But we can see the impact this particular case has had on consumers. It seems that all products of this ilk are now "safety-protected" to assure the consumers of their safety for their products. But more than forty cases of this type had been reported in Chicago (Holmes and Holmes, 2001b).

Psychotic

The psychotic mass killer suffers from a severe break with reality. He may hear voices or see visions. He is different from the psychopath who suffers no remorse, has no social conscious, and is often above average in intelligence (Cleckley, 1941). In the interviews we have done with several serial killers—Ted Bundy, Henry Lucas, John Wayne Gacy, and some others—we are convinced they were psychopaths (Holmes and Holmes, 2010; Rule, 1983). They all lacked feelings for others. When interviewed (San Quentin Prison, June 1985), the Sunset Strip Killer, Douglas Clark, crushed a drinking cup and threw it on the ground. He said that he gave no more feeling about the people he had killed than the cup he just threw to the ground.

Netter (1982, 155) mentions three main characteristics of the psychotic person:

■ Grossly distorted perception of reality
■ Moods, and swings of moods, that seem inappropriate
■ Marked inefficiency in getting along with others and caring only for oneself

There are several reasons that this type of killer is in the minority of mass killers. Actually, in the research we have done, this is probably the mass killer who commits the least number of mass killings. The family annihilator, while usually killing the smaller number at each occurrence, commits the most acts of mass murders (Holmes and Holmes, 2001b).

Conclusion

There is no indication that mass murder will stop. Thirteen mass killers are listed in Table 6.4. They account for ninety-four victims. Obviously, there are more mass murderers than listed and many more across the world. But in this chart we are only interested in the ones in the United States.

Michael McLendon, in March 2009, committed the Geneva County, Alabama massacre. Eleven people were killed including the 26-year-old killer, who committed suicide (Saeed and Alsup, 2009). Chai Vang, an American citizen from Laos, killed six people in a hunting trip in Wisconsin. There was apparently an argument that occurred in the woods over a deer stand. He is currently in prison for his crimes (McFadden and McGuire, 2009).

On April 3, 2009, Jiverly Wong entered the American Civic Association in Binghamton, New York, after blocking the rear exit with his father's car. He entered the facility and killed fourteen people. As the police arrived after receiving a 911 call from a wounded employee, Wong committed suicide. His friends said that Wong was a soft-spoken, nonviolent person with a minor police record. He did say that he wanted to assassinate President Obama and was upset that people made fun of him because of his inability to speak English well. He was a native of Vietnam, but a naturalized American citizen (Branigin, 2009).

On January 30, 2006, Jennifer San Marco shot to death her next-door neighbor. She then went to her former place of employment and killed six workers there. She then committed suicide. There was no certified reason for her killings, but neighbors stated that she was upset with some workers at her former place of employment where she was fired. San Marco had a history of strange behavior, and it was her mental problems that apparently led to her retirement from the post office in 2003 after six years of employment. At that time, she moved to New Mexico. There, she attempted to start a publication, *The Racist Press*, in 2004, but did not have a license. Those who attended a meeting with her at the time recalled that she sat mumbling to herself in a way that sounded as if she were two people arguing. And there were other issues: she would stare at people, and once she showed up at a local service station unclothed (Ramsland, 2009).

Discussion Questions

1. Why is there little or no protection against the actions of the mass killer? Discuss this question with your class.
2. What are the relationships between the mass killer and the victims?
3. Discuss each type of mass killer as indicated in the text. Look at the case of Charles Whitman. What type would he be? Why?
4. Select two types of mass killers. Develop a chart to see the differences. Share this chart with the class.
5. Why do you believe that most mass killers either commit suicide or force the police to kill them at the scene?

References

Armas, G. (2009). Pa. man kills 3, himself, wounds 9. *The Courier-Journal*, August 4, A-8.

Branigin, W. (2009). Gunman kills at least 13 in Binghamton, N.Y. *Washington Post*, April 3.

Breo, D., and Martin, W. (1993). *The crime of the century*. New York: Bantam Books.

Chua-Eoan, H. (2008). Top 25 crimes of the century: Richard Speck. *Time*. http://www.time.com/time/2007/crimes/9.html.

Cleckley, H. (1941). *The mask of sanity*. St Louis: Mosby.

Dietz, P. (1986). Mass, serial, and sensational homicides. *Bulletin of the New England Medical Society* 62: 477–491.

Gresko, J. (2004). 20 years later, San Ysidro McDonald's massacre remembered. *North County Times*. http://www.nctimes.com/news/local/article_2ba4343e-7009-54ce-98df-79a23ff8d0d7.html.

Holmes, R., and Holmes, S. (2001a). *Murder in America*. Thousand Oaks, CA: Sage.

Holmes, R., and Holmes, S. (2001b). *Mass murder in the United States*. Upper Saddle River, NJ: Prentice Hall.

Holmes, R., and Holmes, S. (2010). *Serial murder*, 3rd ed. Thousand Oaks, CA: Sage.

Lalich, J. (2004). *Bounded choice: True believers and charismatic cults*. Los Angeles: University of California Press.

Lavergne, G. M. (1997). *A sniper in the tower*. Denton, TX: University of North Texas Press.

Levin, J., and Fox, J. A. (1985). *Mass murder: America's growing menace*. New York: Plenum Press.

McFadden, C., and McGuire, B. (2009). Spree terrifies small Alabama town. *ABC News*, March 11 (accessed June 22, 2009).

McGinnis, J., (1984). *Fatal vision*. New York: Signet.

Netter, G. (1982). *Explaining murder*. Cincinnati, OH: Anderson Publishing.

Ramsland, C. (2009). *Going postal*. New York: Doubleday.

Robbins, W. (1986). The loner: From shy football player to "Crazy Pat." *The New York Times*, August 22.

Rule, A. (1983). *The stranger beside me*. New York: Signet Books.

Ryzuk, M. (1990). *Thou shalt not kill*. New York: Warner Books.

Saeed, A., and Alsup, D. (2009). Gunman in Alabama slayings was briefly a police officer. CNN, March 3.

Sharkey, J. (1990). *Death sentence: The inside story of the John List murders*. New York: Signet Books.

Smothers, R. (1989). Disturbed past of killer of 7 is unraveled. *New York Times*, September 16. www.statesman.com/specialreports/content/specialreports/whitman/documents.html

Suggested Reading

Douglas, J., and Olshaker, M. (1999). *The anatomy of motive*. New York: Scribner.

Kelleher, M. (1998). *Murder most rare: The female serial killer*. Westport, CT: Praeger.

O'Brien, D. (1985). *Two of a kind: The hillside stranglers*. New York: New American Library.

Rule, A. (1987). *Small sacrifices: A true story of passion and murder*. New York: New American Library.

Chapter 7

Parents Who Kill

Introduction

America is always shocked when a story emerges that a parent has killed a child. Ernie Allen (personal communication, January 2008), the director of the National Center for Exploited and Missing Children in Washington, DC, estimates that about two-thirds of all children killed annually are not killed by sadistic pedophiles but by their own parents. (See Table 7.1 for the demographics of parents who kill their children.) In October, 1994, we all reacted with horror to the story of Pauline Zile's daughter Christina who was reported missing from a flea market women's restroom. After missing for four days, the police discovered blood in Zile's apartment. The story emerged that the child's stepfather, John, beat Christina and stuffed a towel into her mouth. The child went into seizures and died. The parents kept the child's body in a closet for four days. The police arrested the couple and charged them both with murder. Both will spend the rest of her life in prison (Jacobs, 1998).

KILLER PROFILE
Name: Susan Smith
Born: September 26, 1971
Conviction: Two counts of murder of her sons, ages 3 and 1
Sentence: Life in prison
Incarcerated: Correctional institution

Table 7.1 Demographic Data for Parents Who Kill

	Mothers	*Fathers*
Mean age	31	38
Married	70%	80%
Separated	20%	10%
Employed	30%	90%
Criminal History	10%	25%
Mean age of victim	5.8 years	7.9 years
Attempted filicide	<1%	65%

Source: Friedman, S., Hrouda, D., Holden, C., Noffsinger, S., and Resnick, P. (2005). *American Academy of Psychiatry and the Law* 33(4): 496–504. (With permission.)

Shortly after that murder, Susan Smith of South Carolina appeared on national TV in October 1994 crying and pleading with an unknown abductor to return her two sons, ages 3 and 1. She stated that her and the children were abducted in their car by an unknown black man who drove away with the children still in the car. Smith later confessed to letting her car roll into a lake; the bodies of the children were found inside the car.

Why did Smith kill her two children? One theory holds she was in love with a wealthy man in the local area who did not want a woman with children. Another theory expresses the thought that Smith suffers from a mental illness. Regardless of the reason, Smith was sentenced to life in prison for the murder of the children. But Smith did not disappear in the prison setting. She was disciplined for having

WARNINGS MISSED IN BABY'S DEATH

Otty Sanchez, a schizophrenic with a history of hospitalizations, was not taking her medication after suffering from depression after her baby's birth. Despite alarming behavior on her part to her family, she was allowed to have access to a samurai sword.

On July 26, 2009, her screams alerted the police to her plight. She was screaming that she had killed her 3½-week-old son. Sanchez remained hospitalized for a few days recovering from self-inflicted cuts to her torso and an attempt to slice her own throat. Sanchez told the police that the devil made her kill her son and eat parts of her only child.

Source: Roberts, M., and Weber, P. J. Associated Press, July 29, 2009.

sex with two prison guards. She also placed an ad on WriteAPrisoner.com, which has been removed (Associated Press, 2000; Montaldo, 2009).

What is the extent of women who kill their children? Korbin (2002) estimated that between three and five children are killed by their parents every day in the United States. She also adds that approximately 200 women kill their children annually. Thus, homicide emerges as one of the leading causes of death of children in the United States. The Centers for Disease Control states that homicide is the fourth lading cause of death for children under the age of 14. It is the second leading cause of death for children 15 to 18 (Centers for Disease Control, Table 32, p. 190). The statistics suggest that children under the age of 5 are more likely to be killed by their parents, a departure from the commonly held belief that sex-crazed pedophiles are children's main enemy. Women who suffer from postpartum depression who kill their children often suffer for psychosis and report seeing religious symbols and a desire to harm their newborns (Korbin, 2002).

What would cause parents to kill their own child? There are several reasons and theories for such an act. Sarah Hrdy offers one explanation. It may also be that most human mothers rear their children without support and for a longer period of time than other primates. It takes so much longer for humans to function on their own and to be able to care for themselves. The stress becomes long lasting and painful for women who are alone without assistance and human approval. Human mothers are usually sensitive to how much social support they are likely to have and why the mothers are prone to abandon babies and commit infanticide (Hrdy, 1999).

KNOWN OR SUSPECTED FILICIDES

Ivan IV of Russia (Ivan the Terrible) killed his son and heir to the throne in a fit of rage.

Peter the Great of Russia had his son tortured to death, being present at several of the torture sessions and allegedly participating in some of them.

Josef and Magda Goebbels poisoned their six children near the close of the Battle of Berlin in 1945, before committing suicide.

Ptolemy XII of Egypt had his daughter Berenice IV and her husband beheaded in 55 BC. This was after she had dethroned him and poisoned her sister, Cleopatra VI.

Motown singer-songwriter Marvin Gaye was shot to death by his father on April 1, 1984.

Professional wrestler Chris Benoit killed his 7-year-old son Daniel, along with his wife and himself, on June 23, 2007.

Too, we have all heard the stories of stepmothers and stepfathers who kill. Holmes and Holmes (2001, 129) report that stepparents account for a small percentage of parents who kill. But what is especially alarming are the cases where the stepfather physically and sexually abuses the child and then kills the child while the biological mother remains silent. Her motivations for silence may be that she weighs the alternatives of telling the authorities. Can she give up a home for herself and perhaps her other children? Is she frightened for her own safety, afraid that he will harm her too? This mother if faced with a decision: the children or the husband. For most of us the choice is clear and simple. But for some this decision is very complicated. Holmes and Holmes (2001) stated that this decision becomes even more complicated with a mother who suffers from a low self-esteem and is older, thus her life choices are more limited.

Why Do Parents Kill?

Is there such thing as a mother's innate love? Or should it should be seen as a cultural and social response? There are some societies in poverty that kill their babies as sacrifices so that older children may survive. Historically there are some societies where mothers killed their children because they believed the children were meant to die. The babies were not human beings only objects and "temporary household guests."

Men and women may kill their children for different reasons. For example, women are commonly thought to kill their children because the child is unwanted, as a mercy killing, because of some type of mental illness on the part of the mother, because of physical abuse, or as a means of retaliation against the spouse. Fathers who kill murder for different reasons and are also different in the manner in which they kill their offspring. They are more violent in their killings: drowning, shaken, beaten, poisoned, stabbed, and suffocated. Mothers, on the other hand, are more apt to "swaddle" their victims (J. Farmer, interview, Louisville, Kentucky, 2009) and dispose of the bodies close to the home. Fathers, conversely often dispose of their victims sometimes hundreds of miles from the kill site (Holmes, 2009).

Resnick (1969) list several motives for filicide: (1) altruistic, (2) acutely psychotic, (3) accidental filicide (fatal maltreatment), (4) unwanted child, and (5)

DIANE DOWNS: KILLER OF HER CHILD

On a late spring night, May 19, 1983, Diane Downs drove down a dark and lonely rural road outside Springfield, Oregon, along with her three children. Downs stopped her car and shot her three children; one, Cheryl, age 8 was killed; Danny, age 3, was partially paralyzed; and 7-year-old Christie who would be also paralyzed on one side of her body.

Diane, in her late twenties, drove to the emergency room at the McKenzie-Williamette Hospital, walked through the double doors of the emergency room, and announced that her children had been shot. The nurses, doctors, and staff rushed to their aid, but Christie was already beyond any medical aid. Diane herself had been superficially shot in the arm, treated, and released.

Diane's story was that a "shaggy-haired stranger" stopped the car and shot the three children inside the car. The police investigation showed that blood was spattered on the inside of the car and on the windows. But something did not seem right and their investigation continued.

After a thorough investigation Diane was found guilty in the shootings of her children based in part on the testimony of her daughter Christie. Transferred to a prison in New Jersey, she was found to have had sex with a prison guard and in 1994 was transferred again to a prison in California.

On December 9, 2008, Downs had her first parole hearing. Still denying her guilt, she stated that a "bushy-haired stranger" shot her and her three children. She has allegedly changed this story several times, sometimes saying two men wearing ski masks or a corrupt politician shot them. Her parole was denied. Originally given a life sentence plus 50 years, it is doubtful that Downs will be free anytime soon. Called a criminal psychopath, her chances for a successful parole hearing appear slim (Million, 1999; Painter, 1989; Rule, 1987). She is eligible for parole again in two years.

In prison at the Oregon State Prison in Salem, Oregon, Downs met alleged serial killer Randy Woodfield. They fell in love and decided to hold a press conference to announce to the world their engagement. The press met with them in a classroom located between the men's and women's prison. Downs was the first to arrive, and announced it to the press. Woodfield then arrived and was upset that she was the one to announce their upcoming engagement, and he broke off the engagement. Shortly after that, Downs broke out of the prison and was missing for several days before she was apprehended and sent back to the institution. (R. Woodfield, interview, Salem, Oregon, 1985)

spouse revenge. Altruistic filicide is murder committed out of a sense of love to relieve the real or imagined suffering of the child. Acutely psychotic filicide arises when a parents is in the midst of a psychotic episode.

Postpartum psychosis is another emerging offered rationale for a mother killing her children. It may be that some mothers undergo a severe break with reality after giving birth. What makes this defense so difficult for many to believe is that the depression is temporary and by the time the case goes to trial, the depression has been treated and no longer visible. The psychosis takes many forms. One mother who killed claimed that she was possessed by the devil and was made to kill by the devil himself. There is also the case of Mary Anne Stewart, who lived in Louisville,

Kentucky, with her two sons and husband. Stewart was a woman who believed that she was Mary, the mother of Jesus. Her one son was in prison but the second child was 6 years old. Since she was Mary, the son was obviously Jesus. On Good Friday morning, the neighbors on either side of her house heard the young son screaming. They looked out into the backyard and saw Stewart crucifying the small child on two pieces of crossed wood. The neighbors called the police, the police arrested Stewart, and she was charged with physical child abuse. The judge granted her probation under the condition she receive counseling. Less than six months later, the boy drowned in a lake; Stewart believed he could walk on water. She held his hand as they walked across the pond. As they both sank, she was above the level of the water but the small child was below water level; but she kept walking and did not attempt to stop and raise him. In her mind, he was Jesus and he could walk on the top of the water if he only chose to do so. She was again arrested and was sent to a hospital for the criminally insane. After she regained her competency, she stood trial, and was sent to prison, charged with involuntary manslaughter. She received a fifteen-year sentence and is still in the local women's prison.

From various studies it appears the most common reason a mother kills her child is out of a sense of altruism (Goldman, 2007). Women too kill their children because they believe they are ending the pain and the suffering their children will undergo later in their lives (Goldman, 2007). The least common reason to kill

SELECTED CASES OF FATHERS WHO COMMIT FILICIDE

In Montclair, New Jersey, Thomas Reilly decided to kill his family and then killed himself. Reilly drowned his two daughters, ages 5 and 6, in the family's bathtub. He later hanged himself in the basement of the home (Goldman, 2007).

Kevin Morrissey shot his wife and two daughters in a parked car on the street in Berkeley, California, before shooting and killing himself (Goldman, 2007).

In Mobile, Alabama, a shrimp fisherman, Lam Luong, tossed his four young children into a river off a bridge. There was no motive given by Luong in his confession given to the police. He committed the crime in 2008 and was sentenced in 2009 to death by lethal injection (Associated Press, 2009).

In Northampton, England, 33-year-old Gavin Hall killed the family's two cats and his daughter when he found out that his wife was sending sexually explicit e-mails to her lover, a part-time judge. Motivated by a failing marriage and stating that he had an abnormality in his brain, did little to reduce his sentence from the court, a death sentence (Martin, 2009).

In Lancashire, England, Mohammed Riaz killed his wife and four daughters in a house fire that he set. He later died in the hospital. He was convinced that his wife was about to leave him (Martin, 2009).

the child involves revenge (Jefferson County [Kentucky] Annual Report, 2009). Certainly there are parents who blend into more than one category.

We should also be aware that often when a father kills a child, it is often accompanied with a motivation of getting back at the mother. Additionally, when the father kills, it may be accompanied by the father committing suicide. In some extreme cases, the father may kill the entire family including the family pets (familicide). Wrestler Chris Benoit killed his wife and 7-year-old son in their home in Fayetteville, Georgia. The wife and son were apparently dead for several days before the wrestler decided to kill himself. The motive was never found (Goldman, 2007, 1).

FAMILIAL KILLING TERMS

Fratricide and sororicide—Killing of one's sibling
Infanticide—Killing of an infant from birth to 12 months
Patricide and matricide—Killing of a parent by his or her child; the converse of filicide
Prolicide—Killing of offspring
Uxoricide—Killing of one's wife

When men kill their children and the mother of the children, there is oftentimes the thought that money is a motivating factor. He considers himself to be the breadwinner and may believe that his role is greatly suffering and the only way to diminish his feelings of loss of power is to kill the family and commit suicide (Goldman, 2007, 2). In other words he is not only trying to diminish his own pain but also the pain of the family. Mental illness often plays a vital role in the decision to commit filicide (Liem and Koenraadt, 2008). Regardless, there is no single attribute that would account for the decision on the part of the husband to sacrifice his children as well as killing his entire family (West, Friedman, and Resnick, 2009).

From the information in Table 7.3, it is apparent there is evidence that women are more likely to experience nonfatal intimate partner violence. The Bureau of Justice Statistics (2007) reports that on the average from 2001 to 2005, 22 percent of nonfatal violent victimizations were against females age 12 and older. Four percent of nonfatal violent victimizations were perpetrated against males age 12 or older.

But we should not confuse the numbers to account for seriousness. Just because there are less mothers or children killed by the other parent should not lessen the seriousness of either's victimization.

Mothers Who Kill

When mothers kill, there are obvious differences in the methods and reasons. (See Table 7.2 for a list of mothers who have killed.) There are some occasions when a man accompanies the mother in the killing of the child. For example, in 1996, Amy Grossberg and boyfriend, Brian Peterson, cooperated in the death of their baby. Grossberg gave birth to her child assisted by Peterson in a Comfort Inn in New Jersey. Grossberg stated that Peterson dumped the body into a dumpster, but the cause of death was determined by a medical autopsy to be the result of several head fractures and shaken baby syndrome. Peterson was sentenced to two years in prison. Grossberg was sentenced to two and a half years (Wecht, 2007). Because of the killing of this baby, New Jersey passed the Amy's Law bill.

An apparent mental illness resided in the minds of twins, Jane Hopkins and Nancy Byrd. In 1997 Hopkins, 41, stabbed her 9-year-old son and 5-year-old

Table 7.2 Selected Mothers Who Killed Their Children Now on Death Row in the United State

Name	Victim(s)
Kenisha Berry	Smothered 4-day-old son with duct tape
Patricia Blackmon	Killed 2-year-old adopted daughter
Dora Durenrostro	Killed two daughters, 4 and 9, and son, age 8
Susan Eubanks	Killed four sons, 4, 6, 7, 14
Teresa Lewis	Killed husband and 26-year-old son
Debra Jean Milke	Killed 4-year-old son
Frances Newton	Killed husband, 7-year-old son and 2-year-old daughter. She was executed in 2005.
Darlie Routier	Killed two sons, Damon and Devin
Robin Row	Killed husband, son, age 10, and daughter, 8
Caro Socorro	Killed three sons, ages 4 ,6, 9
Michelle Tharp	Killed 7-year-old daughter
Caroline Young	Killed 4-year-old granddaughter and 6-year-old grandson

Source: Friedman et al., 2005.

Table 7.3   Homicide Victim/Offender Relationship by Victim Gender, 1976–2005

	Percent of Homicide Victims by Gender	
Victim/Offender Relationship	*Female*	*Male*
Intimate	30.1	5.3
Other family	11.7	6.7
Acquaintance/known	21.8	35.5
Stranger	8.8	15.5
Undetermined	27.7	37.1

Source: Bureau of Justice Statistics, *Intimate Partner Violence in the U.S.,* 2006.

AMY'S LAW

New Jersey passed House Bill A-6, The New Jersey Safe Haven Protection Act, which allows a parent or a designee to anonymously deliver a baby thought to be under 30 days of age to a police station or an emergency room in a hospital with no questions asked.

daughter, and then stabbed herself with the same knife. Three years earlier, Byrd tried to kill herself and her two children with an overdose of drugs. Friends and neighbors stated that they never saw any signs that the twins had any type of mental illness that would cause them to behave in such a fashion.

In perhaps one of the more bizarre cases of child murder occurred with the case of Marie Noe. Over a period of nineteen years, 1949 to 1968, one by one each of her ten children died. In 1999 when she was 70 years old, she was sentenced to 20 years of probation and 5 years of house arrest. The court psychiatrist determined that she suffered from mixed personality disorder (MPD). He stated that she did not need counseling, but the judge ordered it anyhow (Glatt, 2000).

Andrea Yates became a household name in 1994 when she called the police and confessed that she had killed her five children: Noah, 7; John, 5; Paul, 3; Luke, 2; and Mary, 6 months. She drowned them in the bathtub. The reason? After the birth of her first son, Noah, she started to experience hallucinations and auditory delusions of Satan speaking to her. She explained to the police that each of the children had the mark of the beast (666) under their hair, and she was trying to save them from going to hell before they got older. Yates is presently in a mental hospital for the criminally insane in Texas where she will probably be for a long period of time.

Marybeth Tinning, born in 1942, was married in 1965 to her husband, Joe. She had eight biological children and one adopted child. Her first six babies died of which the local physicians thought to be meningitis, or Reyes syndrome, or sudden infant death syndrome. However, when she brought the adopted child, Michael, to the hospital dead, the doctors then concluded that the deaths were not genetically related. And three years later, the last baby was discovered dead by a neighbor who also happened to be a practical nurse. Given a long prison sentence she will be eligible for parole again in 2011 (Eggington, 1989). According to the New York Department of Correctional Services, Tinning is serving her prison sentence at Bedford Hills Correctional Institution.

Darlie Routier killed two of her children. In 1997, the Texas court found her guilty of one murder and sentenced to death. She is now on death row. This case is currently being reviewed and there is a chance that she may win a new trial. In the original trial, Routier was judged guilty because of her behavior. She failed to try to stop the bleeding of one of her sons, was seen joking at her sons' funerals, and did not behave "as appropriate" according to the investigators. The boys died of deep knife wounds to the chests and punctured lungs (Davis, 2000). In November 2008, a federal judge ordered her case to be reviewed allowing new evidence to be introduced and because of the advances in forensic sciences in the last ten years.

In Louisville, Kentucky, Hope Corwick, age 35, had been left alone with her two children when her husband, an electrical helper, committed suicide. Her husband, Chris, left a message that he was tired of living, disappointed with his work, his life and suffered from depression. He stated that he loved his wife and children and believed that this was the best way to deal with his depression. Corwick had been complaining of being eaten by parasites and also blamed herself for her husband's suicide three years earlier. She said that she gave him parasites, which made him take his own life. On November 6, 2008, Corwick's parents came to her home to take the children away from her and make her seek counseling for her delusional thoughts. They found her on the bedroom floor with a gunshot wound to her head. Before taking her life she stabbed to death both of the children, Emily, age 9, and Lindsey, age 8. One was found on the floor next to the bed and the younger girl was found on the bed. She claimed that she had given her daughters the parasites and had to kill them (Jefferson County [Kentucky)] Coroner's Office, 2009). The autopsy showed that Corwick was negative for drugs.

Corwick's note said:

> I regret this—I know it makes no sense. All of the problems—Chris taking his life wasn't because he was depressed, he was truly sick. I gave him parasites (pinworms). I infected him and the girls. I know I will never be forgiven. Chris deserved a life different. Chris was good, smart, and I didn't deserve him. Also L. (the younger daughter) fell as a toddler walking. I'm sure that explains her behavior and it was my

neglect. I can never say sorry enough. I would not take the girls away from all the friends and family if they didn't have the parasites.

I can never say sorry enough—but you know that Chris loved you all and that the girls will be with there [*sic*] daddy again.

Please have an autopsy so you know that I am not making the parasites up. The girls belly problems, headache, itchings [*sic*], make you toxic and you want to end it all. (Jefferson County [Kentucky)] Coroner's Office, 2009)

As we can see from the words in the suicide note, the mother was convinced that she was killing her children out of a sense of love. She wanted to spare them of any problems that were associated with the parasites. The autopsy showed no presence of any form of parasites.

A more psychodynamic approach is offered by Papapietro and Barbo (2005) as to why parents kill their children. Papapietro and Barbo stated that parents who kill have severe lapses in ego control. This lack of ego control makes it possible for primitive violence to emerge that result in the killing of the child. After experiencing their work in a psychiatric hospital working with mothers who kill, they believe that murder emerges in a psychotic episode often in an attempt to save the child from some sort of cataclysm in the child's future. The authors also state that their own research points out that there are certain "necessary (ego) functions achieved developmentally and incrementally, there is new and evolving neurological research to support the psychodynamic concept of object consistency." Object consistency is the cognitive ability that all allows an infant to maintain the positive concept of the primary parent, in their absence and despite discomfort, frustration, or rage. One reason there may be this inability to establish this object consistency is an injury to the front lobe of the brain that controls certain behavioral functions.

The Victims of Children Killed by Parents

According to the Bureau of Justice Statistics (2007):

■ The number of black children killed by their parents have recently declined, reaching the lowest level recorded in 2004
■ The number of white children killed by their parents have remained relatively stable
■ The number of children of other racial groups killed by their parents have remained the same

Regarding the first finding, it is seen from Figure 7.1, the rate of homicidal incidents have remained higher for blacks than other races at least since 1975. Beyond race, what could be some possible reasons for these differences? Is there a subculture of violence that extends from parent to child in a urban and lower class area, not assuming that all children who are killed are killed by parents from lower class areas? Gun

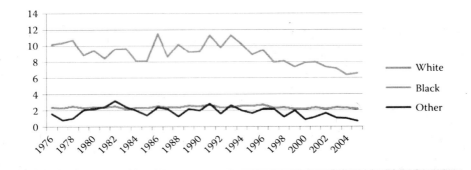

Figure 7.1 Homicide Victimization Rates for Children under Age 5 by Race of Victim, 1976–2005. (Bureau of Justice Statistics, 2007).

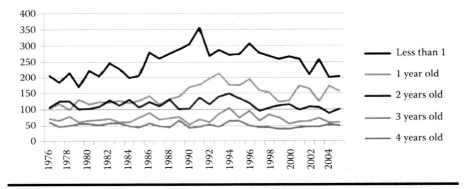

Figure 7.2 Homicides of Children under Age 5 by Age of Victim, 1976–2005 Number of Victims. (Bureau of Justice Statistics, 2007.)

availability is a constant regardless of social class. The pressures that rise from socioeconomic conditions certainly can put personal, social, and mental strains among some parents who are unable to have the resources to turn to for relief.

The age of the child-victim certainly plays a role in the parents' victimization of their children. Illnesses, operations, and injuries certainly take their toll on all parents, and this may be true with the age group of less than age 1, is consistently higher than the other ages under 5. Of course, the younger the child, the more defenseless is the child (Figure 7.2).

Of all children under age 5 murdered from 1976 to 2005 (also see Figure 7.3):

- 31 percent were killed by fathers
- 29 percent were killed by mothers
- 23 percent were killed by male acquaintances
- 7 percent were killed by other relatives
- 3 percent were killed by strangers

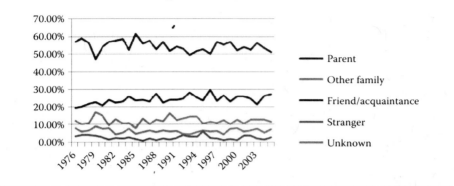

Figure 7.3   Homicides of Children under Age 5 by Relationship with the Offender, 1976–2005 Percent. (Bureau of Justice Statistics, 2007.)

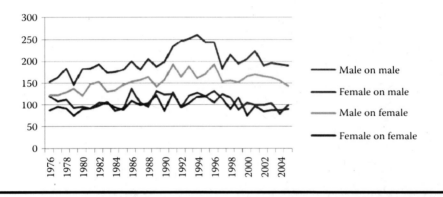

Figure 7.4   Homicides of Children under Age 5 by Relationship with the Offender, 1976–2005 Number of Victims. (Bureau of Justice Statistics, 2007.)

Of those children killed by someone other than their parent, 81 percent were killed by males.

From Figure 7.4 it is apparent that males are the most typical child-murder offender. They are also more likely to kill their male children. Women on the other hand are less likely to kill, but they too are more likely to kill the male child than the female child.

In looking at the data from 2000 to 2005 (Table 7.4), it is evident the male is more likely to kill the male child. In 2005, 36 percent of the time, the male child was killed by the male adult approximately 37 percent of the time. The female killer on male victim, while smaller, the percentages remain about the same since 2000 at about 30 percent. The female on female relationship also has remained slightly about the same, from 13 percent to 17 percent in 2005.

Table 7.4   Infanticide by Gender of Victim and Offender

Year	Male on Male	Female on Male	Male on Female	Female on Female
2000	205	105	166	75
2001	224	100	170	97
2002	190	100	166	84
2003	196	104	163	87
2004	193	79	156	87
2005	191	100	144	90

Source: Bureau of Justice Statistics, 2007.

Conclusion

We must spend time, effort and money to try to find reasons why parents kill their children. Be it genetically determined, a combination of inheritance and environment, social experiences only, or whatever, there has to be reasons and we as a society must try to learn the reasons and do something to stop it. Children are products of their parents and parents certainly have something to do with the formation of children's personality and thus their behavior. Additionally, children are, or at least should be, considered to be an asset to the society and this family. It may be true that the family is the cradle of violence, but it is also the cradle of love and support. And children are a product of the family and the outcome of love within the family. We owe them that.

We were not able to ascertain completely the prime reason for parents killing of their children. We did note that fathers and mothers kill for different reasons. We also briefly examined familicide, and noted that men are more apt to commit this type of murder than do females. Part of the reason may be that men typically use more traditional and deadly weapons, not pills and poisons in their demise of the family.

We have found that fathers are more likely to kill a male child than mothers, and children killed by their fathers average about 6 years of age, about two years older than children killed by their mothers. We also found that mothers tend to be more psychotic than their male counterparts and less likely to kill themselves. Sometimes mothers kill their newborn child in an attempt to hide the birth of the child. In Louisville, Kentucky, a 15-year-old gave birth to her child in the school's bathroom. She said that she did not know that she was pregnant, and after she gave birth, she tried to flush the baby down the toilet. In another case, a young college coed also gave birth to a baby. A member of the school hockey team, she gave birth to the baby in her dorm room at the college. Her roommate reported her to the campus security. She was then arrested and after almost of a year of investigation, she was placed on probation for her crime. This appears to happen mostly to young women, often high school and college-aged females.

Discussion Questions

1. In your thinking and what you have read, what are some of the main reasons parents kill their children?
2. What are the main differences between mothers who kill and fathers who kill?
3. What steps could society and government take to reduce the number of children killed by their parents?
4. What should be the punishment for parents who kill? Normally they receive an extended prison term and released after serving a part of their sentence. What happens in your state?
5. If you are a parent, have you ever had thoughts of hurting your child? How did you handle those destructive feelings?

References

Associated Press. (2000). Second prison guard arrested for sex with Susan Smith. September 26.

Associated Press. (2008). *Man throws 4 kids off coastal bridge.* January 10.

Bureau of Justice Statistics. (2007). *Homicide trends in the U.S. infanticide.* Washington, DC: U.S. Department of Justice.

Centers for Disease Control. (2007). Washington DC.

Davis, D. (2000). *Hush little babies: The true story of a mother who murdered her own children.* New York: St. Martin's True Crime Library.

Eggington, J. (1989). *From cradle to grave: The short lives of Marybeth Tinning's nine children.* New York: William Morrow and Co.

Friedman, S., Hrouda, D., Holden, C., Noffsinger, S., and Resnick, P. (2005). Filicide-suicide: Common factors in parents who kill their children and themselves. *American Academy of Psychiatry and the Law* 33(4): 496–504.

Glatt, J. (2000). *Cradle of death.* New York: St. Martin's Press.

Goldman, R. (2007). Familicide: Why parents kill kids and themselves; Wrestler's death turns spotlight on family murder-suicide. *ABC News,* June 25. http://abcnews.go.com/US/story?id=3307902&page=1.

Holmes, R. (2009). Investigative reports of deaths, Louisville, KY (unpublished paper).

Holmes, R., and Holmes, S. (2001). *Murder in America.* Thousand Oaks, CA: Sage.

Hrdy, S. (1999). *Mother nature: A history of mothers, infants and natural selection.* New York: Pantheon.

Jacobs, M. (1998). Requiring battered women die: Murder liability for mothers under failure to protect statutes. *Journal of Criminal Law and Criminology* 88(2): 579–660.

Jefferson County Coroner's Office. (2009). Annual report. Louisville, KY.

Korbin, J. (2002). American Anthropological Association, press release, March 25.

Liem, M., and Koenraadt, F. (2008). Filicide: A contemporary study of maternal versus paternal child homicide. *Criminal Behaviour and Mental Health* 18(3): 166–176.

Martin, L. (2009). Fathers who kill their children. *The Observer* 45(2): 1–5.

Millon, T. (1999). *Personality guided therapy*. New York: John Wiley & Sons.

Montaldo, C. (2009). *Susan Smith—Profile of a child killer: The tragic South Carolina case of the murders of Michael and Alexander Smith*. http://crime.about.com/od/murder/a/susan_smith.htm (accessed July 17, 2009).

Painter, J., Jr. (1989). The 1980s. *The Sunday Oregonian*, December 31.

Papapietro, D., and Barbo, E. (2005). Commentary: Toward a psychodynamic understanding of filicide—beyond psychosis and into the heart of darkness. *Journal of American Academy of Psychiatry and the Law* 33: 505–508.

Resnick, P. (1969). Child murder by parents: A psychiatric review of filicide. *American Journal of Psychiatry* 126: 73–82.

Roberts, M., and Weber, P. J. (2009). Warning signs missed in baby's death. Associated Press, July 29.

Rule, A. (1987). *Small sacrifices*. New York: Signet.

Wecht, C. (2007). *Mortal evidence: The forensics behind nine shocking cases by Cyril Wecht, MD, JD*. New York: Prometheus Books.

West, S., Friedman, S., and Resnick, P. (2009). Fathers who kill their children: An analysis of the literature. *Journal of Forensic Sciences* 54(2): 463–468.

Suggested Reading

Morton, E., Runyun, C., Moracco, K., and Butts, J. (1998). Partner-suicide involving female homicide victims: A population-based study in North Carolina, 1988–1992. *Violence and Victims* 13(2): 91–106.

Rekers, G. (1995). *Susan Smith: Victim or murderer?* Lakewood, CO: Glenbridge Publishing.

Russell, L., and Stephens, S. (2000). *My daughter Susan Smith*. Brentwood, TN: Authors Book Nook.

Chapter 8

Violence in the Workplace

In Glasgow, Montana, an unidentified attacker went into the Frances Mahon Deaconess Hospital. He shot and killed Melissa Greenhagen, a 37-year-old part-time emergency medical technician. He also shot two bystanders—a hospital nurse and her husband. Both were in stable condition and are expected to survive. The shooter was later killed in a shootout with the police.

—The Courier Journal, **January 19, 2009, A-3**

Introduction

The workplace is supposed to be a safe place, a place where we should be able to spend a great part of our day involved in the economic institution, and a place where we should be in a sense of peace and contentment and not worry about injuries and death.

However, Waddington, Badger, and Bull (2006) report a sense of growing paranoia and ongoing anxiety regarding workplace violence. According to Handgun-Free America (2004), from 1998 to 2003 the number of workplace shootings incidents as well as the number of people killed has increased significantly. The report also found:

- From 2002 to 2003, the number of workplace shootings increased from 25 to 45, and the number of victims killed increased from 33 to 69
- In at least 13.4% of the cases reviewed, the shooter had a history of mental illness

Table 8.1 Domains or Places Where Workplace Violence Occurs

Domain	Percent of Frequency of Occurrence
Taxi driving	23%
Tavern/liquor stores	19%
Convenience stores	17%
Fast food restaurants	17%
Healthcare facilities	10%
Business offices	6%
Government offices	5%
Police work	4%
Post offices	3%
Schools	1%

Source: O'Connor, T. (1997). Social correlates of workplace violence. *Journal of Security Administration* 20(1): 28–39.

■ 91.6 percent of the shooters were males
■ 78.5 percent of the guns used in the workplace shootings were handguns
■ 35.8 percent of all shooters committed suicide after the killing their coworkers compared to 7.1 percent of the female shooters
■ California and Florida were the most dangerous states when it comes to workplace shootings

Statistics and Stories of Murder and Violence in the Workplace

The National Institute for Occupational Safety and Health (NIOSH) defined workplace violence as any physical assault, threatening behavior, or verbal abuse occurring in a work setting (Table 8.2). It includes almost everything but terrorism. NIOSH reports that every year about a million employees are murdered or injured and 1,000 are victims of a homicide. But there are other kinds of violence that is exhibited in the workplace that accounts for days lost at work, pain and suffering, lost wages, and lower productivity. Violence such as unarmed physical attack, stabbings, and rape are perpetrated by other employees, relatives

Table 8.2   Levels of Personal Violence in the Workplace

Level 1
Refuses to cooperate with immediate supervisor
Spreads rumors and gossip to harm others
Belligerent toward customers/clients
Makes unwelcome sexual comments
Level 2
Argues increasingly with customers, vendors, coworkers, and management
Refuses to obey company policies and procedures
Sabotages equipment and steals property for revenge
Verbalizes wishes to hurt coworkers and/or management
Sends sexual or violent notes to coworkers and/or management
Sees self as victimized by management ("me" against "them" mentality)
Level 3
Frequent displays of intense anger resulting in:
• Recurrent suicidal threats
• Recurrent physical fights
• Destruction of property
• Use of weapons to harm others
• Commission of murder, rape, and/or arson

Source: Baron, S. (1993). *Violence in the workplace: A prevention and management guide for business.* Ventura, CA: Pathfinder. (With permission.)

of employees, customers, ex-customers, visitors, robbers, and other strangers. Approximately 60 percent of nonfatal acts of violence are committed by people who are known to the victims, and the other 40 percent are committed by strangers (O'Connor, 1997).

Holmes and Holmes (2001, p. 156) and the National Crime Victimization Survey report:

■ The most common type of workplace violence is simple assault with an estimated 1.5 million assaults occurring each year. U.S. residents also suffered

51,000 rapes and other sexual assaults and about 84,000 robberies while they were at work.

- Annually, more than 230,000 police officers became victims of a nonfatal violent crime while they were on duty.
- Women were more likely than men to be victimized by someone they knew.
- Approximately 12 percent of the nonfatal violent workplace crimes resulted in an injury to the victim. Of those injured, about half received medical treatment.
- Intimates (current and former spouses, boyfriends and girlfriends) were identified by the victims as the perpetrators of about 1% of all workplace violent crime.

SELECTED CASES OF DEATH IN THE WORKPLACE

Archbald, PA—Deborah Bachak, a security guard at Lockheed Martin plant, was shot and killed by a former employee of the plant. The shooter, George Zadoinny then killed himself.

Atlanta, GA—John Henderson, a bartender in the Grant Park area, was shot and killed execution-style at the bar where he worked, the Standard Food and Spirits.

Binghamton, NY—A man went into a refuge aid organization office and killed 13 people and then killed himself. The gunman was found dead in the room with 12 people he had killed.

Boone, NC—Jimmy Roberts, a pawnshop employee, was found shot to death when the police went to the store to check on him when he did not come home from work.

Boston, MA—A Boston crossing guard was struck by a car as she was helping a student cross the street. Marie Conley was killed on the job.

Elmont, NY—Michael Xavier, 43, a livery driver, was found fatally shot in a vacant lot, an apparent victim of a robbery.

Greensboro, NC—Mike Ali, an employee of a local grocery store, was shot and killed during an armed robbery of the store.

Los Angeles, CA—Three gang members have been charged with murder in the shooting death of James Shamp, a bowling alley employee who was empting trash in the alley behind the bowling alley.

New Albany, IN—One person was found dead in the parking lot at the Pillsbury plant. A man has been arrested after a shooting.

Norfolk, VA—Mike Laktami, a 32-year-old cab driver, died after being shot once in the head. He was found sitting in his cab behind the steering wheel.

Raleigh, NC—Howard Palmer, a cab driver, was shot and killed by an unknown assailant.

Silver City, NM—Janvier Ramos, 16, an employee at McDonald's, was stabbed three times by another employee, Judy Maldonado. No reason was given for the killing.

West Covina, CA—A CHP officer, Joe Sanders, was killed when a car ran over him as he was talking to a driver whose car he pulled over for a traffic violation.

Who Are the Perpetrators?

Larry Hansel had been laid off from a San Diego–based electronics company, went into his former employer's company armed with guns and homemade bombs. He found two coworkers and killed one. One was a vice president and the other a sales manager. He was sentence to life in prison. He shows no remorse and had told a *USA Today* reporter that if he had the chance he would do it again (Armour, 2004).

Joseph Wesbecker, suffering from a complex of mental illnesses, went into his former place of employment in Louisville, Kentucky. Placed on administrative leave for his disability, he came to his former workstation armed with several guns. Stepping off the elevator, he killed his first victim, Sharon Needy. Sharon, a former friend of one author (RMH), came in early that day to take an extended lunch hour (Figure 8.1).

On January 23, 2009, a middle school seventh-grader was taken into police custody after stabbing the principal several times in the back with a pencil. The principal, Rob Stephenson, was treated at a nearby immediate care facility and released back to school that afternoon. The youth was charged with assault on a school official. The principal was responding to a call to a disruption in the classroom when the assault occurred.

In examining the information compiled by the Bureau of Justice Statistics, a profile is developed as to the traits and characteristics of the perpetrators of workplace violence. In most cases of workplace violence there is only one perpetrator. If the perpetrator is a male, two of three are strangers to the victims. In slightly less than one in three (29 percent) the perpetrator is an acquaintance. In less than 4 percent the perpetrator is unknown. With the female perpetrator the profile is different. In 47 percent of the cases, the female perpetrator is a stranger. This compares to 65.9 percent of the males. When the female is the killer and an acquaintance, the number is 46 percent compared to 29 percent of the males. Most of the shootings (56 percent) occur in an urban area (Bureau of Justice Statistics, 2009).

A surprising finding was reported. In most cases, in almost 3 out of 4, there was no weapon involved. When there was a weapon, a firearm was the weapon of choice. The second weapon of choice was a knife (Bureau of Justice Statistics, 2009).

Figure 8.1   A murder victim of Joseph Wesbecker. (Photo courtesy of Jefferson County, Kentucky, Coroner's Office).

Who Are the Victims?

What should be remembered when we discuss the traits of the victims of the perpetrator of violence in the workplace is that this type of offender does not have an ideal victim type as does the serial killer. In most cases the victim just happens to be in the wrong place at the wrong time. He may simply be in the way of getting to the real targets. For example, in the Wesbecker case, Sharon Needy just happened to be at the entrance of the elevator talking with a receptionist. She was really not even supposed to be at work that day; she switched days off with another employee. She was in the aisle that led to the manager's office. The manager was out of town that day.

As stated earlier, the victim is often a stranger. Needy did not know Wesbecker. The victims at McDonald's in California did not know James Oliver Huberty. It does not depend upon hairstyles, or color, race, or body build. The person goes into the workplace looking for someone, oftentimes a supervisor or manager, and if someone else is there, that person will suffice.

Four of ten staff and students who witnessed 20 people being gunned down at Dawson College in Montreal in September 2006 have reported mental health

Table 8.3   Murder Victims of Joseph Wesbecker

Name	Age
Richard Bragger	54
William Gannett	46
James Husband	47
Paul Sale	60
Sharon Needy	49
James Wile, Sr.	56
Lloyd White	42

Source: Holmes, R., and Holmes, S. (2001). *Murder in America.* Thousand Oaks, CA: Sage, 163. (With permission.)

problems while others experienced posttraumatic stress syndrome (Arrowsmith, 2009a). Thus we can say that the effects of workplace violence are permeating the psyche of many who have undergone the violence in the workplace. Some report that the bully in elementary school is not any different from the bully in the office (Arrowsmith, 2009b). But victims often do not seek help with any potential psychological problems. Wright (2009) reports:

1. Students needing help were reluctant in getting help because of negative social stigmas.
2. Male support staff was worried of prejudices of mental illness and didn't want to seem weak or vulnerable. They were also reluctant to get help.
3. Groups that had witnessed the shootings were often not offered help and were more psychologically damaged then thought.

We do know that women are more likely to be victimized than men by someone they know. We also know that intimates victimize only about 1 percent of the time. White employees experience workplace victimization at a rate of 25 percent higher than black workers. The profile of the average victim is a white male, 25 to 49 years of age, and the site is a retail sales setting (Table 8.4). In addition, in six cases in ten, the workplace violence is committed by offenders of the same race as the victims.

It is also noted that little research is devoted to documenting violence directed to sex workers as an occupation, particularly prostitution (Monto, 2004). There are obvious reasons for the lack of reporting to the authorities on the part of the prostitute as well as the customer of the prostitute. But does violence occur in this clandestine transaction? Of course. How much? No one knows (Table 8.5).

Table 8.4   Average Annual Number and Percent of Violent Victimizations in the Workplace, 1992–1996

Type of Workplace	Average Number	Percent[a]
Retail sales	292,482	29%
Law enforcement	138,124	14%
Medical	133,012	13%
Mental health	80,771	8%
Transportation	73,894	7%
Private security	61,790	6%

Source: Bureau of Justice Statistics. (2009). *Law enforcement officers most at risk for workplace violence.* Washington, DC: U.S. Department of Justice.

[a] Because of rounding up, percentages do not add to exactly 100 percent.

Table 8.5   Number of Victims in the Workplace, 1992–1996

Type of Victimization	Number	Percent
Homicide[a]	1,023	.05%
Rape and sexual assault	50,500	2.5%
Robbery	83,700	11.7%
Aggravated assault	395,500	21.7%
Simple assault	1,480,000	62.0%

Source: Bureau of Justice Statistics. (2009). *Law enforcement officers most at risk for workplace violence.* Washington, DC: U.S. Department of Justice.

[a] Homicide includes murder and nonnegligent manslaughter.

Occupations and Workplace Violence

The Bureau of Justice Statistics (2009) reports there are occupational differences and exposure to violence in the workplace. At the top of the list are occupations we would expect: law enforcement officers and correctional officers. Taxi drivers and other transportation employees are also frequent victims of violence (Table 8.6).

Edwin Thomas, a New York City bus driver, was stabbed to death on December 1, 2008, after refusing to give a transfer to his assailant, who had not paid his fare. The killer escaped.

On December 16, 2008, in Raleigh, North Carolina, a cab driver was shot and killed in the parking lot of an apartment building.

Table 8.6   Occupation and Average Annual Rate of Workplace Violence

Occupation	Average Annual Rate Per 1,000 Workers
Law enforcement officers	260.8
Corrections officers	155.7
Taxicab drivers	128.3
Bartenders	81.6
Mental health custodians	69.0
Special education teachers	68.4
Gas station attendants	68.3
Mental health professionals	68.2
Junior high school teachers	54.2
Convenience store workers	53.9
Bus drivers	38.2
High school teachers	38.1
Nurses	21.9
Physicians	16.2
All workers	12.6
College teachers	1.6

Source: Bureau of Justice Statistics. (2009). *Law enforcement officers most at risk for workplace violence.* Washington, DC: U.S. Department of Justice.

Police Killed in the Workplace

From 1976 to the year 1998, on average, a law enforcement officer is killed in the line of duty every 57 hours in the United States (Bureau of Justice Statistics, 2009):

- 16 percent were on disturbance calls
- 14 percent were in robbery arrest situations
- 14 percent were investigating suspicious persons/circumstances
- 13 percent were making traffic pursuits/stops
- 13 percent were attempting arrests for offenses other than robbery or burglary
- 10 percent were in ambush situations
- 7 percent were in an arrest situation
- 5 percent were in burglary arrest situation
- 6 percent were in other situations

The statistics also tell us that almost half of the assailants had a prior criminal conviction, and 20 percent were on probation or parole at the time of the death of the officer.

In 2008, there were 127 police officers killed in the United States. Ninety-eight percent were males, had an average of 7.4 years of work experience, and their average age was 40.

From the information in Table 8.7, it is evident that the number one cause of death in policing is auto accidents. Despite the general acceptance that policing is a dangerous occupation and the thought that most police officers are killed in the course of their duties, the dangerousness of their occupation is sometimes the result of their own recklessness.

- Police officer Grant Jensen, St. Charles, Missouri Police Department, was killed in an automobile accident on September 10, 2008. He had been an officer for twenty years. Witnesses said that his car flipped over several times and caught fire.
- Deputy Sheriff Christopher Kane, Jacksonville (Florida) Sheriff's Office, died in an automobile accident when his car ran into the back of a flatbed truck. He had been an officer for twelve years.
- Deputy Sheriff Christopher Yonkers, Barry County (Michigan) Sheriff's Office, died when he had an accident on his motorcycle. He had been an officer for twelve years.

Conclusion

Workplace violence usually commences when an employee has a difficult time responding appropriately to constructive criticism. But the key to lowering and

Table 8.7   Causes of Death of Police Officers, 1998

Causes of Death	Number	Percent
Shot and killed	34	14%
Auto accidents	54	57%
Aircraft accidents	3	1%
Bomb	2	1%
Assaulted	1	1%
Electrocuted	1	1%
Heart attack	6	9%
Vehicular assaults	18	28%
Drowned	1	1%
Duty-related illness	4	1%
Train accident	1	1%
Stabbed	2	1%

Source: Bureau of Justice Statistics. (2009). *Law enforcement officers most at risk for workplace violence.* Washington, DC: U.S. Department of Justice. Percentages do not total 100%.

ultimately eradicating workplace violence is the adequate training of workplace supervisors to recognizing the problem and learning the early warning signs of possible victimization. Education of the workforce is another goal in the lowering of the social problem of workplace violence. We must understand the violent personality and especially those who are violent in the workplace. Workplaces where violence is a strong possibility, workers may experience an ongoing sense of anxiety about potential violence (Waddington, Badger, and Bull, 2006).

It may be that the violent personality suffers from paranoia, but protection must be available for workers. Part of that protection is to alert workers to warning signs. Some signs include the purchase of firearms, the shooter's behavior prior to the shooting, and, oddly enough, an obsessive interest in violence video games (Anderson and Bushman, 2002). Zielinski (2001) urges employers to work with the unions to develop policies that would help workers in their dealings with an employee who might develop violent behaviors. Expanding on these thoughts, Heacox and Sorenson (2004) and Gilmartin and Harris (2001) suggest that an intervention strategy be developed to identify aspects of the work environment that are perceived as obstructive or unsupportive, training employees on the cycle of warnings signs and intervention, establishing a nonpunitive environment and a no-tolerance for bullying behavior, and a screening of applicants for various positions to identify counterproductive behaviors on the part of the employee. Even the employee is requested to submit self-reporting forms that would identify their own aggressive behaviors (Bergman, McIntyre, and James, 2004).

So can there be a profile of a school shooter? From our perspective, we can see that many have a history of suicidal tendencies, morbid fascinations with school shootings, and a lifelong struggle with mental illness. But there are many young people who have suicidal tendencies who not only fail to commit suicide but also do not commit any school shootings. It may be also that many have a fascination with other school shootings but never complete that act. From our perspective, there is no absolute profile that people in the criminal justice system can use to validly predict not only who is a potential shooter but also to recognize when the act is about to occur. "I get a little nervous when people are trying to come up with simple answers, like he was a loner," said Robert Geffner, a neuropsychologist and president of the Institute on Violence, Abuse and Trauma at Alliant International University. "I think every report I've seen is focusing on 'He's a loner.' It would be nice if somebody said, 'Yes he is a loner, but most loners don't kill people.'" (Bryner, 2007). There are, however, a few things that keep resurfacing when scientists review violent and aggressive actions by youth, including depression, anger and resentment, low self-esteem, feelings of victimization and sometimes serious psychiatric disorders (Bryner, 2007).

Discussion Questions

1. Why do you believe incidents of mass murder are increasing in the workplace?
2. In your discussion group, make a list of the various forms of workplace violence.
3. Have you ever been a victim of workplace violence? Please describe. How did it make you feel? What steps did you take to ensure your safety?
4. Pick a case of mass murder in the workplace. Explain why you believe it happened. What could have been done, if anything, to thwart this shooting?
5. Do you believe there is a certain personality type that would be more prone to commit fatal workplace violence? What would those traits be?

References

Anderson, C. and Bushman, B. (2002). The effects of media violence on society, *Science*, March (295) 5564:2377–2378.

Armour, S. (2004). Inside the minds of workplace killers. *USA Today*. July 14.

Arrowsmith, R. (2009a). US mass school-shootings double in a decade, report shows. *Telegraph* (London), July 6.

Arrowsmith, R. (2009b). Workplace bullies: From the schoolyard to the office. *Telegraph* (London), July 7.

Baron, S. (1993). *Violence in the workplace: A prevention and management guide for business.* Ventura, CA: Pathfinder.

Bergman, A., McIntyre, M., and James, L. (2004). Identifying the aggressive personality. *Journal of Emotional Abuse* 4(3/4: 81–93.

Bryner, J. (2007). Scientists: You can't profile school shooters. *Live Science*, April 19, 1.

Bureau of Justice Statistics. (2009). *Law enforcement officers most at risk for workplace violence.* Washington, DC: Department of Justice. (accessed January 15, 2009).

Gilmartin, K. and Harris, J. (2000). Malcontented employees ... what's a supervisor to do? *Police Chief*, December (67) 12: 19–24.

Handgun-Free America. (2004). *Terror nine to five: Guns in the American workplace 1994–2004.* Arlington, VA: Handgun–Free America.

Heacox, N., and Sorenson R. (2004). Organizational frustration and aggressive behaviors. *Journal of Emotional Abuse* 4(3/4): 95–118.

Holmes, R., and Holmes, S. (2001). *Murder in America.* Thousand Oaks, CA: Sage.

Monto, M. (2004). Female prostitution, customers, and violence. *Violence Against Women,* 19(2): 160–188.

O'Connor, T. (1997). Social correlates of workplace violence. *Journal of Security Administration* 20(1): 28–39.

Waddington, P., Badger, D., and Bull, R. (2006). *Violent workplace.* Portland, OR: Willan Publishing.

Weekly toll: Death in the American workplace. (2008). http://weeklytoll.blogspot.com (accessed on January 21, 2009).

Wright, J. (2009). School shootings—why survivors are not likely to seek help. *Examiner. com*, July 6 (accessed July 9, 2009).

www.lineofdutydeath.com (accessed October 27, 2008).

Chapter 9

Rape

Introduction

"He didn't kill me, but he did kill the person I was" (Holmes and Holmes, 2009a). This was a statement made by a woman at a rape crisis center talking with other women who too had been raped. She further added that she was never the same person as she had been before the rape. Her rapist was her boyfriend who believed that her "no" actually meant "yes." Ignoring the twenty women in the group that night, she looked directly at author Ronald Holmes when she added, "A 'no' in a shout or a whisper still means 'no'."

Rape

Rape is a crime of violence and sex is the weapon used (Holmes and Holmes, 2009a). Rape is one means of physical force used by many men to subject women to their whims, desires, and demands.

It is a mistake to believe that only women are raped. Men too are sexually victimized, suffering the same physical and emotional damage as their female counterparts. This is very apparent in today's prisons and jails where the strong victimize the weak and the more vulnerable. The physical damage to the male victim is usually just as extensive as the woman who has been raped and in many cases more so.

Females have long been the target of male victimizations. The supporting role of the female extends to the sexual role. The sexual philosophy as it pertains to women is certainly different than it is for men. Even the sexual positions announce the male superiority. The Bible expresses the importance of rendering the marriage debt. It is a sin to demand the marriage debt but it also a sin to refuse the marriage debt. Either way, sex is seen as bad. But throughout history, males have learned how sex can subjugate, psychologically imprison, and hurtfully control the woman.

Rape as a Weapon

Sex has long been used as a weapon or a reward. A partner who refuses consensual sex to punish one's partner for some real or imagined wrongdoing, is using sex as a tool to punish. On the other hand, sex can also be used as a rewarding tool to reinforce behavior. But at the extreme point of the former example is rape as a damaging agent or as a controlling agent, usually at women.

Why Do Men Rape?

There is no easy answer to the short but complex question of why men rape. It will vary because not all rapists rape for the same reason. Witness the words spoken to one author (RMH) who interviewed a sadistic rapist in one of Kentucky's prison:

> My mother left me on my grandparents' doorsteps when I was 6 months old. My grandfather was a sweet man, loving, caring, and spent no time with me as a child growing up. He was too busy around the house trying to avoid his wife. My grandmother was a domineering, manipulative, hateful woman who could never be pleased by whatever I did. She stood me in corners for even the most minor offense and would whip me with my grandfather's shaving strap, all the time reminding me that I was worthless and a drain to them financially.
>
> I started to work on the streets selling shopping bags when I was 6 years old. I bought them for 3 cents and sold them for a nickel. Other times I shined shoes. By the time I was 10, I caddied and worked the church bingo on Friday nights, and all the while I had to give her half of what I earned. When I came home, she would search my pockets and take what she considered was hers. I soon learned to tell her that I earned less than what I did. I learned the value of a lie.
>
> My first rape occurred when I was 18. She, my victim, was smaller physically than myself, but a year older. I followed her home from a teenage club and attacked her as she was walking toward her home on Hull Street. I was scared later because I thought she would tell her parents. She knew who I was, we had met previously, and we had been on a date a couple times. But she never did. I told her I would kill her if she did. I became reinforced, I believed I could do whatever I wanted and get away with it. I also imagined I was killing my grandmother all

the while. I could not possibly rape my own grandmother, but could someone who reminded me of her.

The rape of this girl was my first. It would not be my last. Her sister was the next. Two years younger, basically the same physical looks, and I followed the same techniques. I told her I would kill her if she told anyone, and she didn't. I wasn't as worried with the second. My last victim, the 135th, was the easiest.

It was probably good that I was caught. I was getting impulses to kill. Had I not been caught, I could be a killer instead of just a rapist.

Yes, my grandmother still visits. She doesn't think I did the rapes. She brings me gifts, makes over me, and kisses me. I think she would have sex with me if I asked. I wonder if she would let me kill her if I asked?

Some of the other reasons men rape include:

Power—One of the historical reasons given for the reason that men rape is for power (Brownmiller, 1975). When a man feels powerless and cannot exert his will in a socially approved fashion, he may try to use force against the weak and the vulnerable of the society: women and children. Brownmiller says rape is about the lack of self-esteem and a deep-seated need to feel some control about oneself. As we said earlier, sex is the weapon used.

The right to control—The rapist uses his power to control others against their will. There are many who believe that women are by nature inferior and if they (the women) cross that line of equality, they need and deserve to be punished. In other words, they need to be put in their place. And from the rapist's point of view, what better way to do that is by forcible rape?

To rid oneself of frustration—In talking with many rapists in prison and on probation/parole, they admit to some sense of frustration prior to the decision to rape. They recount feelings of incidences of anxiety, which they feel can only be relieved by sexual predation. It is not about the sex, because many related that they did not ejaculate during the rape. They may have masturbated later as they recalled their rapes but not during the time.

Biological urges—This may be especially true of the younger male who rapes. This becomes apparent in date rapes when impelled by physical urges and not understanding that a "no" means "no," not a maybe or perhaps. And we must add that a male can stop his sexual act anytime he wishes to do so. He may not be able to stop the ejaculation, but he can stop the act of sexual predation.

Social structural reasons—Some men rape because they think they have the right to put women in their place for their transgressions. Rape in this instance is an expression of the unequal lives of power in a society between men and women. This sense of inequality is not the result of biology but of society. A society that would grant women equal status as men would reduce the rates and numbers of rapes across all age cohorts of women.

The Extent of Rape

Rape is measured is various ways. CEASE (2009) reports:

- In the United States, 1 in 3 women are raped every minute. That results in 78 rapes each hour; 1,872 rapes each day; 56,160 rapes each month; and 683,280 rapes each year.
- 1 out of every 3 American women will be sexually assaulted in her lifetime.
- The United States has the world's highest rape rate of the countries that publish such statistics. It is 4 times higher than Germany, 13 times higher than England, and 20 times higher than Japan.
- 1 in 7 women will be raped by her husband.
- 83 percent of those raped are under the age of 24.
- 1 in 4 college women have either been raped or suffered attempted rape.
- 1 in 12 male students surveyed had committed acts that met the legal definition of rape. Furthermore, 84 percent of the men who had committed such acts said what they had done was definitely not rape.
- 75 percent of male students and 55 percent of female students involved in acquaintance rape had been drinking or using drugs.
- Only 16 percent of rapes are ever reported to the police.

From this information we have seen, we can determine that rape is a huge social issue. To say that one in three American women will be sexually assaulted and one in seven married women will be raped by their husbands is a terrible indictment against men in general and married men in love with their life partner.

According to the FBI, during 2004, approximately 94,635 females nationwide were victims of forcible rape. This estimate represents a small increase of 0.8 percent from the 2003 number and a 4.9 percent rise from the 2000 figure. However, the 2004 data showed a 2.9 percent decrease when compared to the 1995 estimated volume of female forcible rapes.

Source: **Louisville Rape Relief Center 2009**

Table 9.1   Lifetime Rate of Rape and Attempted Rape

Gender and Race	Percentage
White women	17.7%
Black women	18.8%
Asian Pacific Islander women	6.8%
American Indian/Alaskan women	34.1%
Mixed race women	24.4%
All women	17.6%

Source: Louisville Rape Relief Center, 2009.

Almost a third of all women raped are juveniles. In addition, women with disabilities are raped at twice the rate of women with no disabilities. Is it that women with disabilities are less likely to defend themselves and thus more vulnerable targets of physical assaults and rape, or do women with disabilities offer a more despicable target for the frustration of the man who feels compelled to rape?

Concerning men who are raped, the Rape, Abuse and Incest National Network (RAINN) estimates that about 3 percent of American men—1 in 33—have experienced an attempted or completed rape in their lifetime (Tjaden and Thoennes, 1998).

Children

Concerning sexual assault and rape, according to the Bureau of Justice Statistics (2004), victims fall into the following categories:

- 15 percent under age 12
- 29 percent are age 12 to 17
- 44 percent are under age 18
- 80 percent are under age 30
- 12 to 34 are the highest risk years
- Girls ages 16 to 19 are 4 times more likely than the general population to be victims of rape, attempted rape, or sexual assault.

Surprisingly, seven percent of girls in grades 5 to 8 and twelve percent of girls in grades 9 to 12 say they had been sexually abused (Schoen et al., 1997). Three percent of boys in grades 5 to 8 and five percent of boys in grades 9 to 12 say they had been sexually abused. It would appear that many of these young male victims were victimized by pedophiles and hebephiles.

In 1995, local child protection service agencies identified 126,000 children who were victims of either substantiated or indicated sexual abuse (U.S. Department of Health & Human Services, 1995). Of these, 75 percent were girls and nearly 30 percent of child victims were between the age of 4 and 7.

If a child is defined as a juvenile, under 18 years of age, it is truly amazing that three of four children who are sexually victimized are females, and one in three children are between the ages of 4 and 7.

Ninety-three percent of juvenile sexual assault victims know their attacker: 34.2 percent of attackers were family members and 58.7 percent were acquaintances Only 7 percent of the perpetrators were strangers to the victim (Federal Bureau of Investigation, 1996, 2008). The average child victim is a child who lives in an urban/suburban area, under the age of 7, and was attacked by a family member or a family acquaintance.

Victims of Rape

The effects of a rape and sexual assault are grievous. For example, after being victimized, the person is three times more likely to suffer from mental depression than someone who has not been raped. They are more likely to abuse alcohol, more likely to abuse drugs, and more likely to contemplate suicide (Louisville Rape Relief Center, 2009).

Thus, we can see that there are detrimental effects to the rape experience. We have not included one statistic that is often ignored: How many murders have been committed and rape was not included as an official charge? We know from our own research with serial killers that they are known as serial killers and not serial rapists. We know that Ted Bundy killed over thirty women. He was never charged with one rape. John Wayne Gacy killed thirty-three young men; yet, he was never charged with rape.

Rape and the Law

In Old Testament times, women were seen as property, (Deuteronomy 22). In the Old Testament, Moses encouraged his men to use the captured virgins for their own use and sexual pleasure. Moses encouraged his men to kill the male captives and female captives who were not virgins: "But all the young girls who have not known man by lying with him, keep alive for yourselves" (Numbers 31:18). There was also a distinction to be made if the rape occurred in the city or the country. For example in the city, the Bible stated that both the man and the woman should be stoned to death because she did not call out for help (Deuteronomy 22:23–25). If the rape occurred in the country, she was excused from punishment since there would be no one there to hear her. In either case, the father must be compensated because she became "damaged goods" and a less desirable marriage partner.

Rape prosecution in the United States is difficult. Often the victim is again assaulted, emotionally and verbally, by the police and the court system. Despite the rape shield law, which prevents the prosecution from bringing the victim's sexual history in to testimony, the judge and the jury often hear intimate details of the victim's sexual history. This experience can have devastating effects on the victim's self-esteem, reputation, and standing in the community.

The court has to deal with the legal issues of corroboration and consent in rape prosecution cases. The prosecution must prove that a rape indeed did occur, there was sexual penetration, and consent was absent. Some states still require the testimony of an eyewitness other than the victim to secure a conviction. The jury must be convinced that sexual penetration did occur, which demands some type of medical testimony. Detailed medical information is shared with the court on the physical condition of the victim when examined, and the clothing and other personal effects, the presence of semen and blood, and other items must be preserved in some type of "chain of evidence."

As times have changed, so have laws on rape. Some states have moved away from the traditional point of view that sexual penetration is necessary for rape to occur. Oral sex, anal sex, and object penetration are now included in new laws. In some states, resistance does not have to be proven.

In Kentucky, the rape law states:

1. Proof that a sex act has occurred
2. Proof that force has been used
3. Proof that the sex act occurred "without consent"

The reader should consult the rape laws in their own state. However, what we have found is that rape laws are consistent.

Characteristics of Rapists

Rapists are typically young. Four of five rapists are under the age of 30, and 75 percent are under the age of 25 (Holmes and Holmes, 2009a; Queen's Bench Foundation, 1976). Rapists are most often of the lower social class, are often minority group members, and typically choose victims of their own race. Koch (1995), for example, reports that as a rule, blacks choose black victims, white perpetrators choose white victims.

Most rapists are unarmed at the time of their rapes. When the rapist is armed, the weapon of choice is a knife (Bureau of Justice Statistics, 2004; Holmes and Holmes, 2001). It appears that most rapists plan their attacks (Haas and Haas,

2006); fewer than half decide to rape almost instantly. Holmes and Holmes, 2009a report that most rapes of planned. They list some of their findings as follows:

1. Serial rapists traveled an average of 3.14 miles to rape.
2. Half the offenders raped at least once within 0.5 miles of their homes.
3. Those rapists who used a scripted, ritualized type of rape, those who used force, those who burglarized the victim during the rape, and those with extensive criminal records tended to travel farther to find the victim.

Violence during a rape may not be as prevalent as once thought. For example, Stevens (1997) reports career rapists used violence very selectively and sparingly. But the use of violence by the rapist may be connected to the completion of the rape itself. For example, when rape is coupled with the use of alcohol, the likelihood decreased that the rape would be completed, but in those cases that were completed, injury to the victim was more likely (Martin and Bachman, 1998). Hazelwood and Warren (1989) interviewed forty-one rapists in prison and found that the serial rapist more often than not comes from a much different background than many others have reported (Koch, 1995). They offer a profile of a rapist from a married household, intelligent, and well groomed. They added that their pathology is more visible in their early lives. For example, many rapists come from a childhood history of residing in an orphanage, more than 3 out of 4 witnessed sex between their parents, and 1 in 10 living in a foster home as a child.

Other researchers found different results. Vinogradov et al. (1988) studied adolescent rapists and found that many of their rapes occurred toward the end of the family vacation, in their cars, or in the victim's home. Also with this kind of rapist, it was not uncommon to see that they participated in gang-style rapes.

Rape takes many forms. Witness, for example, a power reassurance rapist (Holmes and Holmes, 2009a; Knight et al., 1998). The Villa Anna Rapist in Louisville, Kentucky, broke into a woman's home entering the bedroom window. He forced the young mother back into the bedroom at knifepoint. They sat on the edge of the bed, and he asked her to say the Lord's Prayer with him. He then asked her to please take off her clothing. He then raped her. After he was done, he sat by her side on the bed, and they prayed together, and he asked her another question, "Was I any good?" Playing along with him and she replied "Yes." "Was I better than your husband?" She said, "Much better." He then asked her, "Can I come back again?" She replied in the affirmative. They arranged a time for the next morning at 9:00. The next morning at 9:00, he climbed into the home through the same window in the bedroom. Much to his amazement, the police were waiting for him. He was arrested and later sent to prison for 25 years without the possibility of parole.

By contrast, the behavioral dynamics of the sadist rapist (Knight et al., 1998) is typified by a rapist in a Southern town. He posed as a real estate agent and knocked on the front door of a young homemaker, a mother of three. He asked if he could use her phone; his cell phone was out of power. She let him in. He was dressed in a shirt and tie, and wore the sports coat of a national chain of real estate agents. She turned her back to him as he dialed some numbers on the phone. He silently hung up the phone and walked to her. He placed a knife to her throat and told her, "I know what time Tom [her husband's name] gets home from work. If you don't do what I tell you to do, I will kill Jill when she gets home from St. Albert's School, then I will kill Tommy, he's in the second grade at St. Albert's, correct? And Timmy is in bed right now, right? Timmy is 18 months?"

He had stalked his victim. He knew the names of the children, what school they attended, the name of the infant son and his age. He also knew the husband's working hours and the time he would be home. How did he know that? He had purchased six cheap watches from the local Kmart with minute and hour hands. On randomly selected days he would come by the home early in the morning and place a watch under the husband's rear-passenger-side tire. When the husband would go to work, he would crush the timepiece and show the time the husband left for work. He also visited the business where the husband worked and on randomly selected days, he would also place the watch under the husband's rear-passenger-side tire. When the husband left work to go home, the watch crushed showing the rapist when he retrieved the watch how much time he had to carry out his rape.

All the homes in this upper-middle-class neighborhood had their master bedrooms on the first floor. Each room had a four-poster bed. After the rape, he would force the victim to place herself between the bed poster at the foot of the right-hand side of the bed. She would position herself with her breasts on either side of the poster. He would ask the victim if she had a sewing kit. With a needle and thread, he would insert the needle and thread through the nipples so she would be bound to the bed as he left the scene. He would eventually rape a total of 21 women in this subdivision. He has never been apprehended.

For a more complete discussion of the types of rapists see Knight et al., (1998), Knight and Prentky (1987), or Holmes and Holmes (2008, 2009a).

Conclusion

In looking at the latest data collected by the FBI (2008), it is apparent that the crime of forcible rape has decreased in the last several years:

- In 2007, the estimated number of forcible rapes (90,427) decreased 2.5 percent from the 2006 estimate
- The 2007 estimated number of forcible rapes decreased 3.7 percent from the 2003 estimate and declined 2.9 percent from the 1998 estimate
- The rate of forcible rapes in 2007 was estimated at 59.1 offenses per 100,000 female inhabitants, a 3.0 percent decrease when compared with the 2006 estimated rate of 60.9

■ Based on data reported to the Uniform Crime Reporting Program in 2007, rapes by force comprised 92.2 percent of reported rape offenses, and assaults to rape attempts accounted for 7.8 percent of reported rapes

America's rate of rape will, for whatever reasons, remain one of the highest in the world. We have to ask ourselves why this is the case. Is there something inherent in our society that sees women as chattel, a being to be used, abused, and discarded at the whim of some men? Why are women even in this 21st century still in the minds of many as second-class citizens and less worthy of respect and equal treatment? And what is it about some men who believe they have some type of inherent right to victimize the vulnerable and others who they see as somewhat weak and of less value?

We, as a society, must take some responsibility of protecting those are routinely victimized, those who, by nature of their ascribed status, are targets of victimization and feel persecuted not only by the rapist by also the system that should be more concerned with the protection of the victim and the prosecution of the offender. This should be our focus; this should be our ultimate concern.

Discussion Questions

1. Is rape a sex crime? Explain and defend your answer.
2. What are some things you can do to protect yourself from being a rape victim?
3. Rapists have told the authors that they were exposed to pornography a great deal as a youth but did not feel it caused them to become a rapist. However, pornography taught them some techniques for committing the crime. Defend that position.
4. What is meant by the term *rapist*?
5. What is meant by the statement, "He didn't kill me, but he did kill the person I was."

References

Brownmiller, S. (1975). *Against our will: Men, women, and rape.* New York: Simon and Schuster.

Bureau of Justice Statistics. (2002). *2000 sexual assault of young children as reported to law enforcement.* Washington, DC: U.S. Department of Justice.

Bureau of Justice Statistics. (2004). *2004 national crime victimization survey.* Washington, DC: U.S. Department of Justice.

CEASE. (2009). http://www.ask.com/bar?q=Rape+statistics&page=1&qsrc=2106 (accessed February 17, 2009).

Federal Bureau of Investigation. (1996). Child maltreatment survey 1995. Washington, DC: U.S. Department of Justice.

Federal Bureau of Investigation. (2008). Crime in the United States 2007. Washington, DC: U.S. Department of Justice.

Haas, L., and Haas, J. (1990). *Understanding sexuality.* Boston: Mosby.

Holmes, R., and Holmes, S. (1998). *Serial murder.* Thousand Oaks, Ca: Sage.

Holmes, R., and Holmes, S. (2001). *Murder in America.* Thousand Oaks, CA: Sage.

Holmes, R., and Holmes, S. (2009a). *Sex crimes,* 4th ed. Thousand Oaks, CA: Sage.

Holmes, R., and Holmes, S. (2009b). *Profiling violent crimes: An investigative tool.* Thousand Oaks, CA: Sage.

Knight, R., and Prentky, R. (1987). The developmental antecedents in adult adaptations of rapist subtypes. *Criminal Justice and Behavior* 14: 403–426.

Knight, R., Warren, J., Reboussin, R., and Soley, B. J. (1998). Predicting rapist type from crime-scene variables. *Criminal Justice and Behavior* 25(1): 46–80.

Koch, L. (1995). Interracial rape: Examining the increasing frequency argument. *American Sociologist* 26(1): 76–85.

Louisville Rape Relief Center. (2009). Personal interview.

Martin, S., and Bachman, R. (1998). The contribution of alcohol to the likelihood of completion and severity of injury in rape incidents. *Violence Against Women* 4(6): 694–712.

Queen's Bench Foundation. (1976). *The rapist and his crime.* New York: Wiley.

Schoen, C., Davis, K., Collins. K. S., Greenberg, L., Des Roches, C., and Abrams, M. (1997). *The Commonwealth Fund survey of the health of adolescent girls.* New York: The Commonwealth Fund.

Stevens, D. (1997). Violence and serial rape. *Journal of Police Science and Criminal Psychology* 12(1): 39–47.

Tjaden, P., and Thoennes, N. (1998). *Prevalence, incidence and consequences of violence against women survey.* National Institute of Justice and Centers for Disease Control and Prevention Research. *Washington, DC: Department of Justice.*

U.S. Department of Health & Human Services, Administration for Children and Families. (1995). *1995 child maltreatment survey.*

Vinogravod, S., Dishotsky, D., Doty, A., and Tinklenberg, J. (1988). Patterns of behavior in adolescent rape. *American Journal of Orthopsychiatry* 58: 179–187.

Chapter 10

School Shootings

Introduction

In examining recent school shootings, certain consistent behaviors emerge. A profile can thus be drawn from such an examination. However, not all school shooters fit the profile example.

Females—It is commonly thought that there are no females who are school shooters. In this chapter we will cite at least three cases of females who were involved in fatal school shootings: Laurie Dann, Brenda Spencer, and Doris Young.

White males—The school shooter is usually a white male.

Age—Usually the school shooter is about the same age as the age of the victims. "The older shooters kill older students simply because they themselves are older and further educationally advanced. It is a matter of age of the shooter and the availability of the victims. The middle school shooter kills younger victims simply because younger students attend middle school than high school" (Holmes and Holmes, 2001, 117).

Student—The school shooter is typically a current or past student at the school where the murders occur. Eric Harris and Dylan Klebold were students at Columbine High School in Littleton, Colorado, when they killed twelve students, one teacher, and then themselves at the school (Holmes and Holmes, 2001).

School shooting sites—In suburban or rural communities sites, school killings usually involve multiple victims. In an urban school setting, the victims are usually a personal enemy of the assailant (Holmes and Holmes, 2001).

Middle-class background—School shooters do not come from deprived homes. There are no daily concerns for personal survival (Holmes and Holmes,

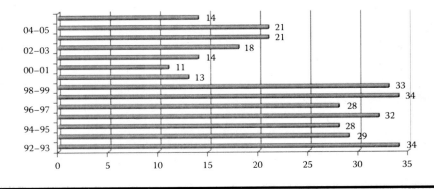

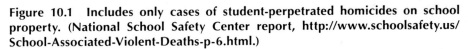

Figure 10.1   Includes only cases of student-perpetrated homicides on school property. (National School Safety Center report, http://www.schoolsafety.us/ School-Associated-Violent-Deaths-p-6.html.)

2001). One killer in Columbine drove a BMW; the other a Honda Accord. One lived in a subdivision of million-dollar houses; the other lived in a subdivision where houses were more modestly priced. The families of the shooters had bought into the American dream. Unfortunately the school shooters did not (Holmes and Holmes, 2001).

Disenfranchised youth—Not all youth involved in school shootings are on the fringe of society. Klebold and Harris were both family members of America's functioning good. One father was an attorney, and the other a local successful community leader. You could make the same argument for a multitude of different killers and their families.

Risk Factors

The Centers for Disease Control identified several risk factors in the early life of the school shooter (Rosenberg, 1999). These factors are broken into four areas:

Individual factors—In this area are conditions not universally accepted by all experts, that show a history of early family aggression.

Family factors—Within the family there is a constant exposure to familial violence; low emotional support to and from family members including parents, and pathology in the family.

Peer/school factors—Negative school peer factors, low to little commitment to the school setting, low classroom settings.

Environmental/neighborhood factors—This includes neighborhoods with high concentrations of poor residents, high levels of transience, high levels of family disruption, low community involvement/participation, diminished economic opportunity, and access to firearms.

If a combination of these risk factors is involved, the propensity of the school shooter personality arises. Unfortunately the exact scheme and arrangements are unknown. What we do know is that school violence is relatively rare in schools. Less than 1 percent of all homicides and suicides among schoolchildren were school associated. However, not all schools are equally affected. Middle schools and high schools in certain impoverished areas are more at risk than grammar schools and private schools with good academic histories ("The facts about school violence," 2000). A thought that many have is that shooters of the school variety are only males. We have found this not to be true in at least three cases as listed in Table 10.1.

Students are less at-risk for incidents of serious violent crime while at school than they are outside of school. Nonviolent crimes such as thefts and less serious incidents such as simple assaults occur more frequently at school (Figure 10.2).

Infamous School Shootings

There have been several school shootings in the last two decades that have galvanized America's attention. The effects of the shootings themselves have been extensive and permeating. One effect is many students refuse to go to school for a long period of time after a school shooting. Perhaps one reason for this is that many seem to have lost the feeling that schools provide a safe haven for students. It has become a place where violence has overtaken the feeling of safety and freedom, and replicates the violent aspects of society. On the microlevel, school shootings can cause posttraumatic stress, depression, and anxiety. Thus the learning process is greatly affected if violent acts occur within the school system.

One of the earliest school shootings occurred in Newburgh, New York, in 1891. James Foster, 70, fired a shotgun at a group of young boys from St. Mary's School, wounding several (*New York Times*, 1891, 2). One of the most deadly school attacks occurred in Bath, Michigan, in 1927. After killing his wife at their home, Andrew Kehoe, 55, set off a bomb at an elementary school that killed forty-five and injured fifty-eight students, teachers, and administrators. Kehoe killed himself as well (*New York Times*, October 9, 1902). Table 10.2 lists other incidents, arranged according to site.

From the data in Table 10.2, school shootings occur with frequency but not regularity. We can determine that there is often there is a copycat killing after a heinous and well-publicized crime.

Holmes et al. (in press) found that in the last two centuries, there have been more than 2,018 cases of school shootings in the United States. The age of the shooters range from the 70s to the preteen years, and in almost every case the

Table 10.1 Ten Myths about School Shootings

Myth	Truth
1. He did not fit the profile.	There is no profile.
2. He just snapped.	Rarely were incidents of school shootings sudden. Most were planned.
3. No one knew.	Before most of the attacks, the shooter told someone about the upcoming attack.
4. He hadn't threatened anyone.	Most attackers do not threaten anyone explicitly. But less explicit works are used to reveal an intention.
5. He was a loner.	Only one-fourth of the school shooters hung out in groups with other "fringe" students.
6. He was crazy.	Only one-third of the shooters had ever been seen by mental health professionals.
7. If only we had a SWAT team.	Most school shooting incidents were over before a SWAT team could arrive at the scene.
8. He had never touched a gun.	Most had an access to a gun and had used them prior to the attack.
9. We did everything we could to help him.	School officials stated that in more than half of the cases they tried to get someone to intervene without success.
10. School violence is rampant.	School shootings are rare.

Source: Adapted from B. Dedman, 10 myths about school shootings, *msnbc.com*, October 10, 2007.

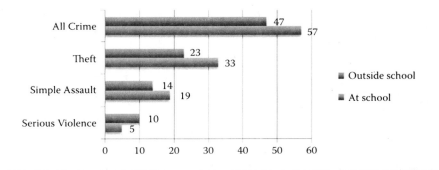

Figure 10.2 School Crime and Safety: 2007. Serious violence includes rape, sexual assault, robbery, and aggravated assault. (National Center for Education Statistics.)

Table 10.2 Selected School Shootings in the United States

Year	State	Attacker	Killed	Injured
Primary and Elementary Schools				
1891	New York	James Foster	0	5
1927	Michigan	Andrew Kehoe	45	58
1959	Texas	Paul Orgeron	6	19
1974	Illinois	Stephen Guy	1	3
1979	California	Brenda Spencer	2	9
1986	Wyoming	David and Doris Young	2	79
1988	Illinois	Laurie Dann	2	6
2000	Michigan	Dedrick Owens	1	0
2001	Pennsylvania	William Stankewicz	0	13
2006	Pennsylvania	Charles Roberts	6	5
2008	Ohio	William Layne	1	2
Secondary Schools				
1940	California	Verlin Spencer	5	1
1956	Maryland	Billy Prevatte	1	2
1971	New Mexico	Michael O'Hearn	1	1
1974	New York	Anthony Barbaro	3	11
1985	Kansas	James Kearby	1	3
1985	Connecticut	Floyd Warmsley	1	2
1986	Montana	Kristopher Hans	1	3
1987	Missouri	Nathan Farris	2	0
1992	California	Eric Houston	4	10
1992	California	John McMahon	2	0
1993	Kentucky	Scott Pennington	2	1
1993	Wisconsin	Leonard McDowell	1	0

(continued)

Table 10.2   Selected School Shootings in the United States (Continued)

Year	State	Attacker	Killed	Injured
1994	Georgia	Brian Head	1	0
1994	Kentucky	Clay Shrout	4	0
1994	North Carolina	Nicholas Atkinson	1	1
1995	South Carolina	Toby Sincino	2	1
1995	Tennessee	Jamie Rouse	2	1
1996	Washington	Barry Loukaitis	3	1
1996	Missouri	Anthony Rutherford, Jonathan Moore, Joseph Burris	3	1
1997	Mississippi	Luke Woodham	3	7
1997	Kentucky	Michael Carneal	3	5
1997	Arkansas	Joseph Todd	0	2
1998	Arkansas	Andrew Golden	0	10
1998	Pennsylvania	Andrew Wurst	1	3
1998	Tennessee	Jacob Davis	1	0
1999	Colorado	Dylan Klebold and Eric Harris	15	24
1999	Georgia	T. J. Solomon	0	6
1999	New Mexico	Victor Codova	1	0
1999	Oklahoma	Seth Trickey	4	1
1999	Texas	Estanislao Balderas	1	0
2000	Florida	Nate Brazill	1	0
2001	California	Charles Williams	2	13
2001	California	Jason Hoffman	5	0
2001	Indiana	Donald Burt	1	0
2001	Michigan	Chris Buschbacher	1	0
2002	New York	Vincent Rodriguez	17	7

Table 10.2 Selected School Shootings in the United States (Continued)

Year	State	Attacker	Killed	Injured
2003	Louisiana	Steven Williams	1	4
2003	Pennsylvania	James Sheets	2	0
2003	Minnesota	Jason McLaughlin	2	0
2004	Washington, DC	Thomas Boykin	1	0
2004	Florida	Michael Hernandez	1	0
2005	Tennessee	Jason Clinard	1	0
2005	Minnesota	Jeffrey Weise	12	0
2005	Tennessee	Kenneth Bartley	1	2
2006	Florida	Chris Penley	1	0
2006	North Carolina	Alvaro Castillo	1	2
2006	Colorado	Duane Morrison	2	6
2006	Wisconsin	Eric Hainstock	1	0
2007	Washington	Doug Chanthabouly	1	0
2007	Massachusetts	John Odgren	1	0
2007	Oregon	Marc Hollingsworth	1	0
2007	Michigan	David Turner	1	1
2007	Texas	Joey Horn	1	0
2007	Oregon	Chad Escobedo	0	10
2007	North Carolina	Josh Cook	1	0
2007	Texas	Allison Camacho	1	0
2007	Texas	Greg Wright	0	0
2007	Wisconsin	Tyler Peterson	7	1
2007	Ohio	Asa Coon	1	5
2008	California	Brandon McInerney	1	0
2008	Tennessee	Jamar Siler	1	0

(continued)

Table 10.2 Selected School Shootings in the United States (Continued)

Year	State	Attacker	Killed	Injured
Colleges and Universities				
1936	Pennsylvania	Wesley Crow	1	0
1949	Ohio	James Heer	1	0
1954	North Carolina	Putnam Davis	1	2
1966	Texas	Charles Whitman	18	31
1970	Ohio	National Guard	4	9
1970	Mississippi	Jackson State Police	2	12
1976	California	Edward Allaway	7	2
1978	California	Theodore Streleski	1	0
1979	Washington	Robert Cutsinger	0	1
1982	Arkansas	Kelvin Love	2	0
1983	New York	Su Yong Kim	2	0
1985	New York	Van Hull	1	4
1989	Washington	Azizolla Mazooni	2	0
1991	Iowa	Gang Lu	6	1
1992	Massachusetts	Wayne Lo	2	4
1995	North Carolina	Wendell Williamson	2	2
1996	California	Fred Davidson	3	0
1996	Pennsylvania	Jillian Robbins	1	1
1996	Indiana	Jarrod Eskew	2	0
2000	Washington	Jian Chen	2	0
2001	Washington	Donald Cowan	2	0
2002	Virginia	Peter Odighizuwa	3	3
2002	Arizona	Robert Flores	4	0
2003	Ohio	Biswanath Halder	1	2
2006	West Virginia	Douglas Pennington	3	0

Table 10.2 Selected School Shootings in the United States (Continued)

Year	State	Attacker	Killed	Injured
2007	Washington	Jonathon Rowan	2	0
2007	Virginia	Seung-Hui Cho	33	25
2007	New Jersey	Jose Carranza	3	1
2007	Delaware	Loyer Braden	1	1
2008	Louisiana	Latina Williams	3	0
2008	Illinois	Steven Kazmierczak	6	18
2008	Arkansas	Kawin Brockman, Kelcey Perry, Mario Toney, Brandon Wade	2	1

shooter was a male. In only three of the cases were the shooter a female. The access to weaponry certainly plays a role in the commission of this act of violence. In many cases the shooters had easy access to guns and other weapons in their homes and from their neighbors. In at least one case, the male was provided a gun from his female friend. In the 2,018 school shooting cases, there were 232 people killed, an average of 2.49 persons killed per school shooting case. Additionally, an average of 4.9 people were injured per episode, which included the students, teachers and administrators, and people in the community.

Outside the United States the statistics and findings are different. For example, outside the United States, from 1850 to the present time, there were 907 cases of school shootings. There were 797 people killed and 1,013 people injured. What is dramatically different is the average number of people killed. In the United States the average number of people killed per incident is 2.49; in other countries the average number killed is 16.6, Accounting for the large difference were several cases of large killings done by the military in three countries. Also in foreign countries, the average age of the killer was 18.9, lower than the U.S. average of 21.6.

Conclusion

There is no verifiable and reliable research that suggests that school shootings will be completely eradicated. It is also true that school shooters are not confined to the United States. Our research indicates there are other examples of school shooters in Japan, England, Russia, Ireland, Iran, Iraq, and many other countries. School shooters often commit their acts out of frustration, reaction to the bullies, or stressors within the family. School violence is a multifaceted reaction to a complex issue that at present had no adequate explanation. There will be continuing acts of school violence in our educational system, from grammar schools to universities. There is no apparent temporal pattern to these incidents, but there does seem to be a pattern that emerges that when one occurs, another, perhaps copycat episode, will follow.

Discussion Questions

1. Why do you think there was an apparent rash of school shootings in the latter part of the last decade?
2. Pick one school shooting. Look at the perpetrator(s). What could have been done to predict such an act?
3. Can something be asserted about pairs in school shootings? Can the formation of a duo add to the act of school shooting?
4. Can we expect to see more future acts of school violence? Or do you think there will be a decrease in school shootings? Why?
5. Compare and contrast the school shootings in the United States and Canada, between the United States and United Kingdom.

References

Holmes, R., and Holmes, S. (2001). *Mass murder in the United States*. Upper Saddle River, NJ: Prentice Hall.

Holmes, R., and Holmes, S (2009). *Profiling violent crimes: An investigative tool*. Thousand Oaks, CA: Sage.

Rosenberg, M. (1999). *Statement on school violence*. Paper presented to the House Committee on Education and the Workforce, Hearing on School Violence, Subcommittee on Early Childhood, Youth and Families, Washington, DC, March 11.

Schoolmaster kills pupils. (1902). *New York Times*, October 9.

The facts about school violence. (2000). www.indiana.edu/~safeschl/facts.html.

Chapter 11

Hate Groups: The Ku Klux Klan, Skinheads, and Other Groups

Introduction

A hate crime is a criminal offense committed against a person, persons, or property that is motivated, in whole or in part, by the offender's bias against a race, religion, disability, national origin, or sexual orientation. This is a simple definition that contains the simple elements. But the crimes are anything but simple and the range of the crimes are immense. The Federal Bureau of Investigation (FBI) (2007) reports:

- In 2007, 2,025 law enforcement agencies reported 7,624 hate crime incidents involving 9,006 offenses
- There were 7,621 single-bias incidents that involved 8,999 offenses, 9,527 victims, and 6,962 offenders
- The 3 multiple-bias incidents reported in 2007 involved 7 offenses, 8 victims, and 3 known offenders

As the FBI indicates, we cannot assume that all hate crimes are reported by the policing agencies across the United States. There are some agencies in law enforcement that do not report for a variety of reasons including one of public relations.

How are hate crimes motivated?

- 50.8 percent were racially motivated
- 18.4 percent were motivated by religious bias
- 16.6 percent resulted from sexual-orientation bias
- 13.2 percent stemmed from ethnicity/national origin bias
- 1.0 percent were prompted by disability bias

As noted, the biases in hate crimes are principally racially motivated. Religion also often plays a role in the commission of hate crimes. Jews are the target in almost 70 percent of hate crimes that are religious based; 9 percent were against Muslims, and 4 percent against Catholics and Protestants.

SEXUAL-ORIENTATION BIAS

59 percent antimale gay bias
24.8 percent antihomosexual bias
12.6 percent antilesbian bias

Source: **FBI, 2007.**

Sexual orientation also plays a role in the commission of hate crimes and most are directed against homosexuals and lesbians.

There are other items that can be considered when we speak of hate crimes. Property crimes, for example, that are hate motivated are most typically directed at individuals (54.7 percent), business or financial institutions (11.5 percent), against the government (7.4%), and religious organizations (6.8 percent; FBI, 2007).

Hate crimes are undesirable and affect a significant number of people, but can be remedied through collective social action. The question becomes, what are we doing about it? Is there enough of our citizens who are willing to attack the issue and get the government, from the lowest level to the highest level, to fight this significant issue?

In this chapter, we will look at several types of hate crimes, each one different, and each one committed in a different manner and with different motives. The Ku Klux Klan (KKK) and skinheads have long been on the forefront in the commission of hate crimes against certain people and groups. Blacks, gays, certain religions including Jews, and now Hispanics are their targets. Perhaps soon certain motorcycle groups will become a group equivalent to the KKK as a hate group. The Hells Angels, for example, is slowly emerging as a significant group that commits all kinds of crimes including hate crimes. We will keep a close watch on their development.

Let us now move into a discussion of the KKK and the skinheads.

The KKK: An Introduction to Two Centuries of Hate

Hate crimes became highly organized in the United States on a spring evening in 1865 in Pulaski, Tennessee, when a small group of six former Confederate soldiers met in the home of one of the men to start a campaign of hatred that would last to the present day. The Civil War had just ended, and looters and criminals besieged the South. Carpetbaggers became an economic blight on the financial health of the South. The South was in a state of social disorganization and mass confusion.

HISTORY OF KKK

Name: Ku Klux Klan
Founded: Pulaski, Tennessee
When: Christmas Eve 1865
Founders: 6 Confederate soldiers
Mission: Maintenance of white race

In two short years, the Klan adopted a more hierarchal mode of operation. This design was akin to the military model that most of its members were used to as former members of the Confederate army. Brian A. Scates was elected as leader and president of the organization. The Klan dogma, the Prescripts, was introduced. The dogma of the early Klan insisted upon white supremacists' beliefs (Ku Klux Klan, 2009).

The KKK started with a mission of achieving white supremacy. The members of the Klan went on a rampage against freed slaves and blacks, white Republicans, and other groups including Jews, Catholics, and gays. Their acts were composed of various forms of violence including murder, burning houses, and leaving the bodies of their victims on the roads (Du Bois, 1998).

To hide their identities while committing their violent acts, Klan members often wore masks and robes. Many were active in their communities, and the apparel was one manner in which to hide their identity. Sometimes, the KKK members offered the story that the men in disguise were the ghosts of Confederate soldiers coming back to this earth to win back the rights of the whites of the South (Foner, 2002).

In 1870, the federal government passed legislation, the Force Acts, that were used to prosecute Klan acts of violence. But the KKK was not the only group that used violence against others. The White League and the Red Shirts also were involved in counts of social and personal terrorism with a particular aim of suppressing the Southern Republican votes. These groups all contributed to years of violence that moved out of the South to almost every state of the Union. There is a professed statement that the Klan does not discriminate against the handicapped. Their statements continue that many of their members have handicaps (www.kukluxklan.bz).

After the turn of the 20th century, the membership of the Klan diminished. At one time, the Klan numbered around 500,000 but quickly dropped. Circa 1915, the "second" Klan was founded and after WWI the social upheaval, poverty, and immigration of Irish, Catholics, Italians, as well as the migration of southern blacks to the northern cities of industry created in the minds of many a feeling that these groups were a drain on the financial resources of the country as well as the employment opportunities for the white population. With the jobs, moneys, and social programs often directed toward these groups, the KKK preached hatred, racism, anti-Catholicism, anti-Communism, and anti-Semitism. The Klan used public lynchings, vandalism, destruction, and cross burnings to intimidate the general public. Its membership rose to more than 4 million members. However, there was no manner in which to verify membership. There were no membership rosters or chapters, and few members were willing to verify their membership in the Klan.

The "second Klan" was much different than the first. It became highly organized with a national center and klaverns (chapters) around the country. With 4 million to 5 million fraternal members at its height in the mid-1920s, the membership dropped sharply to about 30,000 in the 1930s. The second Klan probably reached an all-time low after the Great Depression and WWII.

The name of the Ku Klux Klan is a label that many white supremacist groups had attached to their organizations. However, not all chapters were true members of the Klan. But what they have in common is a terrorist philosophy and an opposition to civil rights and integration. This can best be seen in the 1950s and 1960s in the alliance of white hate groups with the police departments in the South and the politicians such as George Wallace of Alabama. Several members of a KKK-affiliated group were convicted of murder in the cases of Medgar Evers, three civil rights workers in Mississippi, and children. In 2008, federal agents breaking up a plot to kill then–presidential candidate Barack Obama arrested Daniel Cowart, 20, of Bells, Tennessee. He and his alleged partner, Paul Schlesselman, 18, planned to rob a weapons store, then shoot or decapitate 102 black people in Tennessee and then kill Obama (Jordan, 2008).

Today, the Southern Poverty Law Center estimates there are about 5,000 members of these 150 (estimated) klaverns in the U.S. (personal communication, Southern Poverty Center, June 30, 2009).

How does one join the Ku Klux Klan? As with many other organizations, there are stated requirements:

■ You must be a free white male or female of European descent, at least 18 years of age.
■ You must be able to profess Jesus Christ as your personal Savior.
■ You must not be married to or date people of other races, not have mixed-race dependants, this includes adopted children.

- You must agree to conform to the rules of this order, and be willing to swear you will not conspire to commit any crime while a member.
- You must not join us with mercenary intent, or under secret evasion of any sort.
- Under no circumstances will we accept for membership: homosexuals, atheists, or those who have been found mentally insane. We will not accept candidates that have been convicted of treason, or espionage against the United States of America.
- You must be a U.S. citizen. We do not accept foreign nationals, or have foreign members.

Klan Activities

In the early 1900s, the Klan opened klaverns in many states including Arkansas, Texas, Oregon, and California. Aided by the temperance movement, the Klan entered a clandestine battle against taverns and other establishments. They continued to oppose minorities and by 1922 in Oregon, turned their efforts to the eradication of Catholics who comprised about 8 percent of the population in Oregon. Additionally, they favored a bill that required all children to attend public schools.

Two white men in South Carolina were charged with kidnapping and sexually assaulting a 15-year-old black girl and a black woman in what officials described as racially motivated attacks. Police said that one of the two had links to the Ku Klux Klan group.

Source: **Holthouse, 2009, p. 9.**

In Georgia in 1913, Mary Phagan, a young woman employed in a factory managed by a Jewish gentleman, Leo Frank, was found dead after being raped. Frank was found guilty of the crimes and was placed in jail under heavy guard. A small group calling itself the Knights of Mary Phagan broke into the jail after the judge commuted the sentence from death to life in prison. The group lynched Frank using the Klan's Prescripts as a rationale for the acts. Many members of the Knights of Mary Phagan were also members of the Klan itself (Quarles, 1948).

Wearing their robes, masks, and burning crosses in the night, the Klan committed numerous acts of violence. Armed KKK members killed thousands of blacks; Du Bois (1998) estimates that ten to one blacks were murdered as whites. For examples, in North and South Carolina in the latter part of the 19th century in an eighteen-month period 197 blacks were killed and 548 were victims of aggravated assaults (Du Bois, 1998).

Hate in the 21st Century

The time of hate within the KKK has not stopped. (Table 11.1 lists racist groups currently active in the United States.) In 2003, in South Carolina, a "unity" gathering was held in a small retail store packed with racist memorabilia. The shop's owner, John Howard, stated that he has been a member of the KKK for over forty years. The gathering started with a wedding performed by Pastor Jonathon Williams, the leader of the Aryan Nations. The wedding, punctuated by shouts of "Heil Hitler" followed by a presentation by Josh Fowler, the alleged Grand Dragon of South Carolina's KKK, with tales of hate directed toward blacks. Other speakers followed, with hate directed toward Hispanics and blacks as "soulless" mud people (Sugg, 2006).

> In San Antonio, Texas, a judge sentenced Aryan Brotherhood prison gang member Michael McCallum to 18 years in prison for beating to death a man he met at a gas station after the two had an argument about membership in a white supremacist prison gang. Security was heightened during McCallum's trial after a swastika was discovered on a prosecutor's car window.
>
> *Source:* **Holthouse, 2009, p. 9.**

Gays are also being targeted more harshly by hate groups than in the immediate past. The National Association for Research and Therapy of Homosexuality argues gays can be changed with counseling. This group came under extreme fire recently when one of its members, Gerald Schoenewolf, wrote a professional paper that he argued that blacks were better off in slavery than being free. Many members of the association have left it because of the contents of the essay (Mock, 2006).

There has been a great rise in the number of "traditionalist" Catholic groups that preach anti-Semitic hatred. We must remember that it is a small number but nonetheless the groups do exist. One such group is the Catholic Apologetics International (CAI). This group headed by Robert Sungenis. One message is that "the Jews, Judaism, and the land of Israel" are among the major forces aimed at Satan ruling the earth (Bierich, 2006, p. 28). In examining the Web page of the organization, the group advertises many products for sale as well as information about the organization itself. For example, it sells videos, (e.g., *The Papal Infallibility Debate* and *Is Benedict the Pope?*), books (e.g., *Galileo Was Wrong: The Church Was Right*), and articles that reflect the basic philosophy of the CAI.

Another Catholic group that has emerged with a message against the Jews and the gays is the Catholic Counterpoint. It was started by John Maffei, who wrote:

Table 11.1   Alleged and Selected Racist Groups Currently Active in the United States

Acronym	Name	Background
ORION	Our Race Is Our Nation	Christian Identity background
UEHT	Our Honor Is Loyalty	German white supremacist group
UAO	United As One	White supremacist group
CI	Christian Identity	White Europeans are real "chosen" ones
WPWW	White Pride World Wide	White supremacists
SWP	Supreme White Power	White supremacists
ROA	Race Over All	Neo-Nazi white power group
RAHOWA	Racial Holy War	White power over minorities by war
ZOG/JOG	Zionist/Jewish-Occupied Government	Believes Jews control government and finances

I'm an Air Force Veteran, educated under the G.I. bill at a Jesuit college: that taught me the Catholic faith by Intellect [*sic*] alone. Logic, Epistemology, Cosmology and Apologetics … etc, [*sic*] were drilled into my brain day after day until it became a way of life. After college I worked in the motion picture business and got away from the faith. When I, finally [*sic*] got back to the Church: eveery [*sic*] thing that i [*sic*] witnessed was repugnant to what the Jesuits had drilled into my head. So I started to look for the real Catholic Church. Also, when JFK got assassinated, has a good rifleman [*sic*], I knew that something was phony.

So I was pushed by into doinf [*sic*] documentaries on the Catholic Church and the Country that I fought for.

It was, and still is, not easy to seek the truth.

Our contact information

By email:

Jmaffei@verizon.net

Ccp/ P.O. Box 445/ Broomall, Pa 19008

By phone:

610 789 1774 (between 9 a.m. and 9 p.m. eastern)

Maffei also sells soap products and authored a book on how doctors actually make people sick.

Father John O'Connor, another early member of the organization, an avid anti-Semite and Holocaust denier is depicted on the Web site (www.catholiccounter point.com/father-john-o39conn39.html). O'Connor, a Dominican priest, found that homosexuals had infiltrated the seminary in Chicago. He reported this info to the Vatican, thinking that it would take care of the matter, but he was wrong. According to the Web site, O'Connor died before he could get the psychiatric care recommended to him by the Catholic Church.

Another Catholic group is the Slaves of the Immaculate Heart of Mary, based in southwest New Hampshire. Its Web site identifies its founder as Leonard Feeney. In 1953 he died after he was excommunicated from the Roman Catholic Church. The Slaves are anti-Semitic and are opposed to the Catholic Church's efforts to reconcile with the Jews. The Slaves are also opposed to feminists, sodomites, and those who advocate birth control. Brother Francis Maximiliam Maria, age 95, now heads it (www.catholicism.org, n.d.).

There are other churches that can be termed as hate groups. In Burlington, Kentucky, there is the Fellowship of God's Covenant People. The members believe that God chose only white people to become rulers and administrators of God's kingdom on earth. Additionally only white people can have a "personal relationship" with God. They also believe that there are enemies inside the government that have lobbied property taxes, income taxes, and inheritance taxes, all of them against God's laws (Eigelbach, 2005, A1).

The FBI added Edward Eugene Harper, a former member of the antigovernment "Patriot" group, Montana Freeman, to its Ten Most Wanted. In 1994, Harper failed to appear for a court hearing in DeSota County, Mississippi, where he had been charged with sexually molesting two girls, ages 3 and 8, and has been a fugitive ever since. The former truck driver, now 62, has worked as a ranch hand in Wyoming and Montana. [See Figure 11.1.]

Source: **Holthouse, 2009, 9.**

Skinheads

As seen in Tables 11.2 and 11.3, racist skinheads are active in almost every state. There are more chapters in some states than in others, and the Confederate Hammerskins are well represented.

The skinheads originated in England in the late 1960s. They had a "mission" to shave their heads and gather at rock concerts. The social commentators of the time defined them as working-class youth, a reaction to the hippies with their hair cropped closely, wearing work shirts, and short jeans.

FBI TEN MOST WANTED FUGITIVE

UNLAWFUL FLIGHT TO AVOID PROSECUTION - CONSPIRACY TO COMMIT SEXUAL BATTERY, CHILD FONDLING, SEXUAL BATTERY

EDWARD EUGENE HARPER

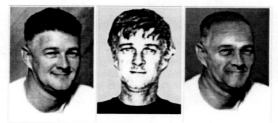

| Photograph taken prior to 1994 | Photograph taken in 1994 | Photograph age progressed in 2008 |

Aliases: Edward E. Harper, Ed E. Harper, Ed Harper, Eddie Eugene Trimue, Eddie Harper, Eddie Eugene Harper, Edward Eugene Trimue, Ed Harmon, Edward Trimue

---

Figure 11.1   Edward Eugene Harper

Description

Date of Birth Used:	March 1, 1946	**Hair:**	Gray/Brown
Place of Birth:	New Mexico	**Eyes:**	Hazel
Height:	5'10"	**Complexion:**	Medium
Weight:	165 pounds	**Sex:**	Male
Build:	Medium	**Race:**	White

Occupations: Semi-Truck Driver, Mechanic, Forklift Driver, Ranch Handler
Nationality: American
Scars and Marks: Harper has a navy/maritime tattoo on one of his biceps. The tattoo depicts an anchor with an entwined snake.
Remarks: Harper reportedly subscribed to Sovereign Citizen ideology and claimed to be a member of the Montana Freemen, a group involved in domestic terrorism activities. He has family ties to Arkansas and may have lived and worked in Wyoming and Montana.

Caution

Edward Eugene Harper is wanted for his alleged involvement in sexual behavior with two girls, ages 3 and 8, in Mississippi. The girls lived near Harper and reportedly visited him at his home. Harper was charged with sex crimes and arrested. Harper was released on bond, but he failed to appear for a court hearing in 1994, and his bond was revoked.

Reward

The FBI is offering a reward of up to $100,000 for information leading directly to the arrest of Edward Eugene Harper.

Considered Dangerous

Table 11.2   Selected States and Skinhead Organizations
California
American Front
Berdoo Skinheads
Confederation of Racialist Working Class Skinheads
Comrades of Our Race's Struggle (C.O.O.R.S.)
Deadline Skinheads/Deadline Family Skins
Florida
American Front
American Nazi
Combat 18
Confederate Hammerskins (CHS)
The Hated
South Florida Aryan Alliance (SFAA)
Vinlanders Social Club (VSC)
Georgia
American Skins
Confederate Hammerskins
Free Your Mind Productions
Unaffiliated Skinheads
Kentucky
Blood and Honour Kentucky
Confederate Hammerskins
Scioto Valley Skinheads
Texas
Aryan Renaissance Society
Aryan Fourth Reich Skins

Table 11.2 Selected States and Skinhead Organizations (Continued)
Confederate Hammerskins
TCB (Taking Care of Business) Hate Crew
Volksfront
Unaffiliated Racist Skinhead Activity

Source: Anti-Defamation League, Racist Skinhead Project (retrieved 5-20-09).

In the early 1970s, the original skinheads had mostly died out and a new group took its place. Its mission statements and activities were directly influenced by the music of the time, punk rock, and took on a racist perspective. Skinhead groups gained acceptance by larger, more organized hate groups such as the Ku Klux Klan, the Church of the Creator, and the White Aryan Resistance. In the mid-1980s, there were 2,000 racist skinheads in the United States. In the late 1990s, there were approximately 3,500 racist skinheads (Neiwart, 2009).

We must be careful not to assume that all skinheads hold the same dogma. There are some skinheads who are not political; their interests are only attuned to music and other forms of the art. For example, Skinheads Against Racial Prejudice (SHARP) was founded in 1987. This organization is opposed to racism and neo-Nazism. Another group of the same ilk is Anti-Racist Action (ARA). What we are interested in this section are the skinheads who are racists and often identify themselves with the adult hate groups.

Skinhead Groups in the United States

Perhaps one of the more formidable and well known of the skinhead groups is the Hammerskin Nation. The group was influenced by Pink Floyd's music, particularly a song about Pink, a down-and-out punk rock singer and drug addict, who loses touch with reality and turns to fascism. He sings a song about lining up all the Jews, gays, and blacks against a wall and shooting them.

Strangely quiet in the last couple of years, the Hammerskin Nation has a long history of violence. The group was founded in Dallas, Texas, in the late 1980s and was known as the Confederate Hammerskins. Since that time, numerous groups have been founded across the United States as well as in other countries including England, France, Spain, the Netherlands, Switzerland, and Germany.

The homepage for the Hammerskin Nation states its mission, an ideology of racial violence and white supremacy. The leadership has changed and the episodes of violent acts have diminished.

Table 11.3 Selected and Alleged Skinhead Groups and Geographical Locations

American Front
Florida
Utah
American Thule Society (ATS)
Pennsylvania
Arizona Hammerskins
Arizona
Aryan Fourth Reich Skins
New Jersey
Blood and Honour
California
Kentucky
Ohio
Confederate Hammerskins
Alabama
Georgia
Kentucky
North Carolina
Florida
Tennessee
Texas
East Coast Hate Crew
Massachusetts
New Jersey
New York

Table 11.3 Selected and Alleged Skinhead Groups and Geographical Locations (Continued)

Eastern Hammerskins
Maryland
New Jersey
Delaware
Pennsylvania
Hammerskin Nation
Oklahoma
Insane White Boys
California
Midland Hammerskins
Colorado
Kansas
Missouri
Northern Hammerskins
Illinois
Michigan
Minnesota
Wisconsin
Northwest Hammerskins
Idaho
Oregon
Washington
Volksfront
Arizona

(continued)

Table 11.3 Selected and Alleged Skinhead Groups and Geographical Locations (Continued)

California
Massachusetts
Oregon
Texas

Source: The Anti-Defamation League, Racist Skinhead Project, (accessed May 20, 2009).

But Hammerskin Nation is not the only group involved in hate crimes. For example, in February 2009, Walter Dille, Jr., 40, was convicted of a murder that was committed in 2005. A member of the Atlantic City Skinheads, he murdered a black woman. He forced her back into her car in a small parking lot and then shot her in the back of her head. In January 2009, police arrested four white supremacists for attempted murder. The men were accused of beating a 19-year-old Hispanic man to the extent that the young man lives in a long-term care facility with brain damage. The four men were alleged members of the C.O.O.R.S (Comrades of Our Race's Struggle Family Skins). In Arizona in December 2008, four members of the Creativity Movement were arrested for two acts of hate crimes. The first case involved a 23-year-old Hispanic male who was wearing an antiracist t-shirt. The four men shouted "white power" and hit the Hispanic in the head with a bar stool. A white woman was punched in the face. In the second case, a 32-year-old black male was beaten and stabbed twice in the stomach that required surgery (ADL, Racist Skinhead Project, and Associated Press, 2009).

In 1998, two men allegedly beat two homeless men to death in Tampa, Florida. The men, Kenneth Hoover and Charles Marovskis, were arrested in 2009 and charged with murder. The men were members of the Blood and Honour hate group and the killings were part of an initiation rite into the group. They beat one man, Alfred Williams, to death with a tire iron, and the second victim, Richard Arsenau, was murdered with an ax. The killers, who pleaded guilty to their crimes, considered the two victims inferior because they were homeless (Mohammed, 2009, A1).

In April 2009, a white supremacist, Richard Poplawski, was alleged to have killed three Pittsburgh police officers. At the time, there was no known motive for the shootings, but informants said Poplawski had in recent months exhibited growing anger at the police and the local government (ADL, 2009). He was reported to be an alleged member of the Stormfront hate group (Neiwart, 2009).

The basic tenets commonly espoused on Stormfront (Neiwart, 2009):

1. The federal government, mainstream media, and banking system in these United States are strongly under the influence of—if not completely controlled by—Zionist interest.
2. An economic collapse of the financial system is inevitable, bringing with it some degree of civil unrest if not outright balkanization of the continental US, civil/revolutionary/racial war, SHTF/TEOTWAKI scenario, etc.
2A. This collapse is likely engineered by the elite Jewish powers that be in order to make for a power and asset grab.

Skinhead hate groups are not confined to males. For example, one singing group, Prussian Blue, is composed of two sisters, Lamb and Lynx Gaede. They sing racist songs whose lyrics speak of honoring Hitler's deputy, Rudolf Hess, and during their concerts they make Sieg Heil salutes. A racist mother allegedly raised them. Lynx stated "We are proud of being white. We want our people to stay white we don't want to just be, you know, a big muddle. We just want to preserve our race" (Curtis, 2005, A1).

The Internet and Hate

The Internet now provides us with a wide array of information that caters to a wide spectrum of interests. The interests include both criminal and noncriminal behaviors: pedophilia, pornography, swinging, prostitution, and information regarding aberrant sexual behavior. It also includes links to homepages for various hate groups including the Hammerskins, Blood and Honour, and the Vinlanders Social Club.

What are some of the benefits belonging to various hate groups in the United States and other countries? Let us list the following:

Economy

The Internet is an extremely economical way to reach millions and millions of interested persons. Messages can be typed in one minute and the messages can be received around the world in seconds. Not only can it be received immediately, they go to audiences that are interested in the topics and the messages offered.

Blogs, Twitters, and Chat Channels

With blogs and chat channels and now Twitters, one can instantly "talk" on the Internet with literally thousands of people who share a common interest on blogs and chat channels. If you are interested in sports, for example, you can access a channel to suit your interest. You can even enter a site that caters to a specific team, for example, the New York Yankees or the Boston Red Sox, the Dallas Cowboys, or the Denver Broncos.

The blog is akin to your own personal newspaper. You can select your topic and change the topic as you wish. Others may respond to the information on the blog. And only the master of the blog can control the topic of the time.

On the chat channels you can easily enter into a dialogue with others who are interested in the same topic. So it goes with skinheads and other hate groups. There can be instant messaging occurring among the various participants online at that time. They can ask questions, secure information, and share common ideas and interests. Someone from France, for example, can instantly communicate with someone somewhere else in the world in an instant.

A Twitter is concerned with topics that people can respond to. Operated by the owner of the Twitter, it differs from a chat channel in the way it is organized around a particular topic and the instant messaging involved.

Immediate Access to the Entire World

There is no other communications media that is more readily accessible to people around the world as the Internet. It is inexpensive and so easily learned that people can master the basic functions of the computer to enter the Internet and exchange messages of hate and distain. E-mail messages can be exchanged instantly, and plans for actions can be sent to others with a touch of a button regardless of the locations of the senders and those who receive such messages.

Educational

The Internet provides instant educational material on varied subjects. At the touch of a button, one can learn the many wives of Henry VIII. At the same time one can retrieve the homepage of the Southern Poverty Law Center, Blood and Honour, Hammerskin Nation, the Anti-Defamation League, and many other groups. One can access several encyclopedic sources in an instant or go to search engines, such as Google, Ask Momma.com, Yahoo, GoodSearch, AOL, and Ask Simon (J. Holmes, personal interview, June 1, 2009). From such vast resources, information is literally at the fingertips of anyone with limited knowledge of the Internet and the way it works.

Finding Others of the Same Interests

In blogs, chat channels, and general homepages, your username is often asked. In this way you become known as someone interested in a certain topic, be it baseball, colleges to apply to for entrance, or hate groups around the world. One can instantly find others who share common interests. One can instantly locate the main homepages for groups with the information one seeks. One used to have to physically go to the university or public libraries and spend the better part of the day; nowadays the same material can be retrieved in a manner of minutes. Moreover, the Web sites will often have names that are up to date, and accompanied by mailing addresses, Web addresses, and phone numbers.

Conclusion

Hate groups in the United States have been active for almost two hundred years. But in actuality, we are certain there have been groups active since early history aimed at destroying certain groups that do not share the same ideology.

As we have seen in this chapter, there are many groups that have been identified as "undesirable" and thus "worthy" victims of violence and even extinction. Those groups include the KKK, skinheads, and many other groups. The acts of violence ebb and flow with time. The group for victimization will change also. Blacks, Jews, Catholics, and gays have historically been the "traditional" victims. During the early 19th century, the Irish came to this country and almost immediately became a target for hate groups. Now, with many Hispanics and other peoples from South America, the Caribbean, and Mexico coming into the country, they are emerging as targets.

The natural question to be asked is whether hate-motivated violence will ever end. Our point of view is that it will not. We believe the targets of violence may change and the methods of violence may change, but there will always be a segment of the population that many will feel are undesirable and unworthy of humane treatment. As a progressive society in the 21st century, we should make every effort to protect those who may be subjected to such acts of violence and, in many cases, fatal violence. In one high school in Louisville, Kentucky, there were two white gangs vying for supremacy. One head of gang A invited the other leader of gang B to join him after school to talk about a merger. He promised him drugs and girls for sex after their meeting was over at a local park. When the second young man arrived at the public park he was shot and killed, a single bullet to the back of the head. The killer was quickly arrested by the local police and is presently awaiting trail (B. Goodall, personal communication, July 31, 2009). These gangs were not organized, but were rather small number of members who preached a message of hate toward others. Only with the help of the school security authorities who were consulted in that district and talking to them about the gang problem and bringing certain items of physical evidence did the case reach a solution. But that school still has a problem with gangs despite the school being located in a "nicer" part of town with a low crime rate. The security guard at that school stated the gang problem at other schools is just as bad if not worse. The guard also stated that he had been at the school since 1993 and the gang problem has only gotten more serious as the time passed with murder being the outcome of only a handful of cases.

Discussion Questions

1. What social and cultural issues were favorable to the formation of the first stage of the KKK?
2. What do you think are some of the most heinous crimes committed by the KKK?
3. Look up hate gangs on the Internet. How many did you get? What were the membership requirements?
4. Could we classify motorcycle gangs as hate groups? Why or why not?
5. Captain Kirk and Mr. Spock have just transported us to the year 2050. What are the statuses of the various hate groups such as the Hammerskin Nation and Blood and Honour?

References

ADL, Racist Skinhead Project, Associated Press. (accessed May 20, 2009).

Bierich, H. (2006). The dirty dozen. *Intelligence Report* 124: 28–31.

Catholicism.org homepage. (2006). http://catholicism.org.

Curtis, B. (2005). Bakersfield girl band: Cute Ku Klux Klan. *One Bakersfield*, April 26.

Du Bois, W. E. B. (1998). *Black reconstruction in America: 1860–1880*. New York: Oxford University Press.

Eigelbach, K. (2005). Church called a "hate group." *Cincinnati Post*, November 5, A1.

Foner, E. (2002). *Reconstruction: America's Unfinished Revolution, 1863–1877*. New York: HarperCollins.

Getler, W. and Brewer, B. (2009). *Shadow of the sentinel*. New York: Simon & Shuster.

Holthouse, D. (2009). The year in hate, 2008. *Intelligence Report*, 133, 9, Montgomery, AL: Southern Poverty Law Center.

Kukluxklan/bx/faq2.com, page 2; (accessed May 8, 2009).

Mock, B. (2006). One more enemy. *Intelligence Report* 124: 14–15.

Neiwart, D. (2009). The emerging portrait of Richard Poplawski: A white-supremacist radical. *Crooks and Liars*, April 5, 1A. http://crooksandliars.com/david-neiwert/emerging-portrait-richard-poplawski- (accessed March 14, 2009).

Quarles, C. (1948). *The Ku Klux Klan and related American radicalism and anti-Semitic organizations: A history and analysis*. Jefferson, NC: McFarland & Company.

Sugg, J. (2006). Aging Aryans. *Intelligence Report* 124: 11–13.

White supremacist kills three officers in Pittsburgh. (2009). ADL.org. http://www.adl.org/learn/default.htm (accessed May 20, 2009).

Suggested Reading

Mock, B. (2009). Hate crime activities. *Intelligence Report.*

Chapter 12

Youth Violence: An Alternative Explanation; The Cultural Transmission Hypothesis

Introduction

Perhaps there is no hotter topic in the area of violence research than that of youth violence. Whereas the rate of overall crime and violent crime in recent years appears to be on the decline, the exact opposite can be said of youth violence. In a recent study conducted in Orange County, Florida, researchers found that despite seeing an overall reduction in number of cases handled by juvenile authorities, the proportion of all juvenile cases that are serious or violent has increased over time. These researchers also found that the proportion of all juvenile cases that are capital crimes or crimes carrying a potential life sentence has increased dramatically in recent years (Adams et al., 2007). The stories across the country are similar. Crimes committed by youth today are quite different than in years past. Traditionally youth committed property crime and engaged in minor assaults between peers. However, today the quantity and qualitative nature of youth violence has changed to reflect the patterns of adult violence.

If you ask any police officer what has changed in the area of crime and violence, they will tell you that they have never seen the type of violence committed by youth that you see today. You have kids killing their brothers, cousins, or friends for very

Michael Eugene Thomas, 15, a ninth-grader at Meade Senior High School in Anne Arundel County, Maryland, was found strangled and barefoot on May 2, 1989. James David Martin, 17, was charged with first-degree murder for killing Thomas, taking his two-week-old Air Jordans, leaving the body in the woods near the school. The shoes cost $115.

small or menial offenses. Many have attributed this trend to back to the early 1990s when teenagers and others were being killed for their Air Jordan shoes. While it is clear that this violence was not the result of anything that Nike or Michel Jordan did in particular; it was one of the first times people began to hear of these senseless acts of violence over such trivial things as tennis shoes.

Presently, kids are killing kids and others not just for shoes, property, cars, or even girls. In one case in Mississippi, an 11-year-old boy got his father's shotgun and shot and killed his 9-year-old brother because he beat him in a video game ("Boy shoots brother," 2009). Although the case was ruled an accidental shooting, why would an 11-year-old kid seek a gun to settle a childish dispute? In another case, an Ohio teenager shot and killed his mother and shot his father when they took away his *Halo 3* video game. Daniel Petric received 23 years in prison for his part in this violent episode. What made the case even worse was that the young man placed the gun in his father's hands after he shot him to make it look like a murder-suicide (Caniglia, 2009). Again, the question is where do these kids learn that it is acceptable to take the life of someone else for something as trivial as having a video game taken away from them? Is it part of our contemporary culture? Is it the media that is transmitting these values to our kids? Or are children simply emulating the behavior of their role models that all too often have frequent run-ins with the law. Examples of this type of senseless crime are endless.

In academe, most criminal justice and criminology programs have classes specifically targeted to crimes and deviant acts committed by youth. They typically define those who commit these crimes as juvenile delinquents. In a broad sense, delinquency in this regard refers to any type of behavior that juveniles commit that violates the norms set by the controlling group (Kratcoski et al., 1990). However, the types of crimes that will be described in this chapter go beyond these stereotypical definitions. We will not be talking about such acts as skipping school, driving a car without a license, taking part in a fight in a schoolyard, or even buying or selling alcohol or drugs. Instead we will be focusing on crimes of violence committed against each other or adults, and how the media and other role models may affect this qualitatively different type of violence.

The Causes of Juvenile Violence

In the past, we have sought to explain youth violence in more traditional sociologi-cal stereotypes. Most of these explanations state that youth get involved in violence because of the pushes and pulls of living in an impoverished environment, or being raised in one-parent families. However, the proportion of juveniles living below the poverty level has declined significantly since its peak in 1993 (Office of Juvenile Justice and Delinquency Prevention, 2008a). Thus, the pains of poverty do not appear in the aggregate to have contributed to this alarming trend. While the num-ber of youth belonging to one-parent families is increasing, this is true of all racial cohorts and not just those belonging to the specific ethnicities. Overall the number of youth living in one-parent families has increased 18 percent since 1960 (Office of Juvenile Justice and Delinquency Prevention, 2006).

Others have sought to explain this escalating level of violence by explaining youth involvement in gang activity and the drug trade. It is said that youth interact-ing with violent drug and gang leaders learn the trade from their interaction with older mentors. There does appear to be some truth to this, since the extant literature does indicate that youth are often recruited to be the drug runners and middlemen between the dealers and buyers. However, many of the youth that get involved in these violent and sometimes fatal episodes are not involved in drugs, gangs, or the culture related to this form of lifestyle.

The data on youth homicide also appear to support this contention given that almost 37 percent of all homicides committed by juveniles also involved another adult offender. This figure was up from 25 percent in the early and mid-1980s (Federal Bureau of Investigation, 2008). Thus it may be that some of the increase in this violent type of crime committed by juveniles may stem from interaction of older, more mature deviant peers. In fact, Blumstein (1995) states that the sharp rise in homicides by juveniles is attributable to the recruitment of juveniles into illegal drug markets.

But the question is, why are our youths so attracted to crime, especially crimes of violence? Traditional theoretical explanations of juvenile violence center on the same or similar causes of juvenile delinquency. Most of these theoretical explana-tions have been influenced by prior research or the eras in which they were devel-oped (Kratcoski et al., 1990). Classical school theories use the works of Bentham and Becarria and state that those who engage in criminal behavior use a weighting process in which the perpetrators weigh the cost of engaging in these forbidden activities against the pleasure or rewards they will receive by do so. If capture or detection was certain, juveniles in this case would refrain from engaging in future acts of delinquency (Bentham, 1830). However, the problem with these theories is that many of these kids appear unwilling or unable to weigh the true cost of their behavior and what it will mean for their future. In fact many children in the inner city who live in impoverished environments are more likely to experience pessi-mism, instrumental helplessness, lethargy, and depression, which often contributes to the lack of hope for the future (Davis & Stevenson, 2006). Thus, if they lack hope, how can these youth help but to live in the moment?

Similarly, theorists belonging to the neoclassical school believe that punishment for crimes that violate the social order must be dealt with harshly and that any unpunished deed becomes a threat to the social order and can lead society to further moral deterioration (Bailey et al., 1974; Wilson, 1975). However, what many of these youth see is that that the rich and famous who commit acts of violence or sexually assault oftentimes go unpunished.

The problem with these theories and their conceptualization of the problem of violence among our youth is multifaceted. First these theories all but ignore the media influences that many of our kids are barraged with on a daily basis. Second, at the time of their writings, kids especially very young children were not being recruited to be drug runners for organized crime and drug racketeers, or play video games daily where they kill opposing soldiers with a variety of guns or other mechanized artillery. And finally, the writers never dreamed that involvement in a life of crime for our nation's youth would be so lucrative in terms of the money that could be made and the status that could be assigned to those involved.

The Cultural Transmission of Values Hypothesis

The aforementioned influences have all changed the nature of the involvement of youth in violent crime and have set the stage for the current period where involvement in crime and living the "NBA lifestyle" appears to be the lifestyle choice among many of the youth both in and outside the inner city. While it is difficult to brand the current lifestyle that many of our youth have chosen as comparable to that of professional athletes, many kids mimic the behavior of the players.

While many professional athletes claim that they do not want or ever asked for this responsibility of being role models, it comes with exposure from the game and other mass media outlets. One does not have to look too far to see the trouble that many of these players have had in their run-ins with the law. For instance, Allen Iverson (Figure 12.1), a point guard with the Philadelphia 76ers, came into the National Basketball Association (NBA) as a first-round draft pick. Within three years he was the leading scorer in the NBA and was named the league's Most Valuable Player in 2001. However, Iverson was also arrested for breaking into his cousin's home with a gun threatening two men while looking for his wife ("Police to ask," 2002). Iverson was charged with fourteen felony and misdemeanor charges including assault and terroristic threatening; however, he was only tried for two misdemeanor counts of terroristic threatening. Iverson's success along with his radical looks (tattoos, braided hair) and gun-toting lifestyle (including the recording of an explicit rap song) was an immediate hit with many inner city youth who wished to emulate his bravado.

Event# 181174087
PID# 948473
Name: IVERSON
      ALLEN
Arrest Date: 07 / 16 / 02
Age at Arrest: 27.
Height: 6'00"
Weight: 165
Hair Color: BLACK
Eye Color: BROWN
Phila PD ARREST Database
Printed 11-HP10-NT1726 07 16 02 16 51

Figure 12.1   Mug shot of Allen Iverson following his arrest in Philadelphia.

Other sports figures, including Ray Lewis (Figure 12.2), the middle linebacker for the Baltimore Ravens, have had run-ins with the law. In February of 2000, Lewis was charged with murder after two men were stabbed to death outside of an Atlanta nightclub after attending a Super Bowl party. Lewis later pleaded guilty to misdemeanor obstruction of justice and was given twelve months probation.

Another prominent sports figure arrested is the former quarterback for the Atlanta Falcons, Michael Vick (Figure 12.3). Vick was indicted in 2007 in Virginia for promoting dog fighting, and torturing and killing animals. He was sentenced

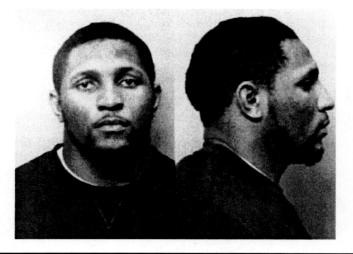

Figure 12.2   Mug shot of Ray Lewis following his arrest in Atlanta in 2000.

Figure 12.3   Mug shot of Michael Vick after his arrest in 2007.

to twenty-three months in prison and was released after serving just a little more than over a year. Upon his release he was reinstated by the NFL and is on the Philadelphia Eagles roster.

In another case in 2008, Plaxico Burress, a standout wide receiver and Super Bowl hero for the New York Giants, walked into the Latin Quarter nightclub in New York City carrying an unregistered and concealed weapon. While he was walking upstairs to the VIP section, his gun accidentally discharged wounding him in the leg. Despite only harming himself, he pled guilty to a weapon charge was sentenced to two years for criminal possession of a weapon.

Whereas the previous examples are sports figures, some in the entertainment industry have also contributed to this culture of violence among our nation's youth. For example, rap star Jay-Z (aka Shawn Carter; Figure 12.4) was arrested in New

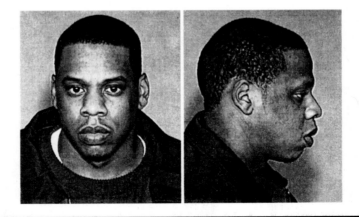

Figure 12.4   Mug shot of Jay-Z following his arrest in New York in 1999.

Figure 12.5   Mug shot of Tupac Shakur following his arrest in New York on sexual assault charges.

York in 1999 for stabbing a record company executive at a downtown nightclub. Jay-Z was charged with felony assault, but pleaded guilty to a reduced count and received three years probation.

Another of the more famous cases of those in the entertainment industry include rapper Tupac Shakur (Figure 12.5). Shakur was convicted in 1994 for the sexual abuse of a female. After he was released, he was murdered in 1996 by an undisclosed assailant.

More recently, hip-hop singer Chris Brown was arrested for assaulting fellow singer and girlfriend Rihanna after they left a party on February 8, 2009. Brown who enjoyed the reputation for being a role model for many African American youth for his clean living and lifestyle had his reputation destroyed after pictures of Rihanna with a black eye appeared. It was reported that Brown and Rihanna had a tumultuous relationship with a history of violence between the two. Brown pled guilty and was sentenced to 5 years of probation, 180 days of community labor, and 52 weeks of domestic violence training (Dillon & Hutchinson, 2009).

While the previous examples of famous athletes and entertainers is not exhaustive and only represents a snapshot of high-profile celebrities that have had run ins with the law, it does show the problem that we have in our society. Although it is true that celebrities and pop icons have historically had unpleasant encounters with the law and legal system, the difference is now that these individuals are treated by many of our nation's youth as royalty. Our youth wear their clothing lines, buy their sports jerseys and shoes, and often listen to their music. Further, celebrity behavior is often perpetuated and transmitted to our nation's youth in music videos and song lyrics. For example, in Shakur's song "Death around the Corner," he describes the need to stay high to survive and keep his finger on the trigger waiting for his enemies to attack.

I see death around the corner, gotta stay high while I survive
In the city where the skinny niggas die
If they bury me, bury me as a G nigga, no need to worry
I expect retaliation in a hurry
I see death around the corner, anyday
Trying to keep it together, no one lives forever anyway
Strugglin and strivin, my destiny's to die
Keep my finger on the trigger, no mercy in my eyes.

While not condemning gangster rap or debating its place as a solid music genera, the ideas and values transmitted by the lyrics do have an impact on those that idolize and follow these entertainers. In fact, when Iverson was set to release his first rap album, NBA Commissioner David Stern stated that the lyrics to his song "40 Bars" were "coarse, offensive and anti-social." In the song, Iverson makes repeated derogatory statements about blacks, gays, and women. In one line Iverson even transmits the message that if you are man enough to carry a gun, you better be man enough to pull the trigger (Sheridan, 2000).

Even though there is anecdotal evidence that many of our nation's youth are affected by the cultural transmission of the values evident by the culture and lifestyle espoused by many of our nation's sports and entertainment icons, there is little evidence to point to a direct correlation or causal relationship.

Historical and Academic Roots of the Cultural Transmission Hypothesis

One of the first to examine this relationship was Patrick Colquhoun, a magistrate in 18th century England. He claimed that crime was on the rise because the morals and habits of the lower class were becoming progressively worse (Radzinowicz, 1956). Colquhoun attributed the transmission of these morals to the explicit lyrics contained in songs by many of the popular entertainers in the local pubs. Although this study is dated, it does show that representations in the media have long been a concern for policy makers and criminal justice officials.

A more recent meta-analysis conducted by Livingstone (1996) found a relationship between the media and glamorous images of offenders. In this study, the researcher found a relationship, but only a weak one. She stated that media does have a dramatic effect on how we look at ourselves even though it is hard to demonstrate or prove. Going further she stated that the enculturation process works over long periods of time contributing to other factors that make us who we are.

However most studies recite the finding of Schramm (1961), which found that the harm of the glorification of violence in the media may affect some youths under some conditions. However, for most children, the images portrayed by television and the media is not particularly harmful or beneficial.

Other researchers have gone further and focused on the roles and responsibilities of the media. For instance, Simon Lee states that the media through the images they portray to the general public are no longer observers or fact reporters, but rather players in the game (Peay, 1998). As players they set the stage for the normative assessments of what it right, wrong, acceptable, encouraged, discouraged, or in some cases socially tolerable.

If the research on the media and transmission of cultural deviant and criminogenic values has taught us anything it is that there is likely to be some effect on some youths, especially those with weak social bonding. These youths are commonly referred to as those who occupy the lower social class who do not necessarily buy into traditional white, Anglo Saxon, Protestant, middle-class values. Hence, if the effect is real, we would expect to see rampant youth violence in impoverished minority youths, typically thought to reside more so in the inner city. Thus we would expect that over time, the rate of violent crime should increase among this population regardless of the overall rate of violent crime.

Using Uniform Crime Report (UCR) data, we see that despite the falling rate of violent crime, between 2003 and 2006 the estimated number of juveniles committing homicide rose 30 percent (Federal Bureau of Investigation, 2008). Further, homicide ranks as the second leading cause of death among people between the ages of 10 and 24. Of those killed, 87 percent were males and 84 percent were killed with a firearm (Centers for Disease Control, 2009).

The Extant Data

If the contention is that those youths who are most affected by the cultural transmission of values from the media and the behavior of those the youths mirror is true we would expect that African and Hispanic youths would comprise the majority of youths who are both involved in homicides as both victims and offenders.

Using data from the Centers for Disease Control we can see that those killed are predominately African American. The Hispanic victimization rate is about a third of that of African Americans and Caucasians barely make the scale. To make this point even clearer, despite the fact that African American youth constitute 16 percent of youth in 2002, the murder rate among this class was more than 4 times that of the majority class (Caucasians) who comprise almost 49 percent of the juvenile population (Snyder & Sickmund, 2006).

Further in a nationally representative study of youths in grades 9 to 12 in 2007, the Centers for Disease Control found 18 percent of youths carried a weapon (gun, knife, or club) to school in the 30 days preceding the survey. What this means is that approximately one to five youths carried a weapon to an educational institution

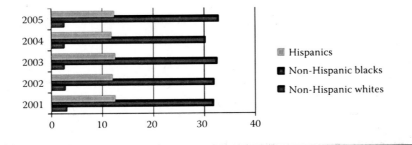

Figure 12.6 Trends in Homicide Rates Among Persons 10–24 Years Old. (Bureau of Justice Statistics.)

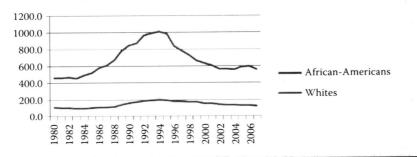

Figure 12.7 Juvenile Arrest Rates for Aggravated Assault by Race (1980–2006). (Bureau of Justice Statistics.)

for either protection or mimicking the behavior of their cultural icons (sports or other entertainment figures).

While the data cited up to now only involves homicides, it is not just homicide that we are concerned with. Youths are involved in a variety of other violent offenses in the streets, their neighborhoods, and in the schools. One of the most common offenses is aggravated assault. Using data collected by the Office of Juvenile Justice and Delinquency Prevention (2008b) we can see that the arrest rate for this type of violent offense was again much higher (on average 3.6 times as much) for African Americans than for Caucasians.

While some argue that African-American youth may be more heavily involved in the crime of aggravated assault, it is difficult to say how much more because African American youths are more likely to be arrested by the police than their Caucasian counterparts. While there my be some truth to this statement, there is some doubt whether the "bias" of our nation's law enforcement agents account for such wide disparities in arrest rates. Zimring (2004) offers another explanation. He states that the simple increase in arrest rates of simple assault or aggravated assault are likely due to changes in law enforcement policy to get tough on violent behavior. In any event, the arrest rates for our nation's African American youths are much higher than for youths in the majority.

Pathways for Further Research

The data presented and available to researchers appear to clearly indicate that African American youths are involved in violent crimes such as homicide and aggravated assault significantly more than Caucasian youths. However it would be disingenuous to attribute this effect to the cultural transmission of the values of the lifestyle of many of their roles models through the media to account for these apparent differences. It is a plausible explanation and surely one that needs to be considered, but not the sole explanation. In fact at this point in our academic pursuit of this connection it would be just as difficult to say that African Americans are more criminogenic than Caucasians. This is because we know there are many more factors that account for these differences than race alone. In fact, the academic literature tells us that such factors as social disorganization, cultural deviance, and strain theory often account for these differences through lack of development of the social bond, economic inequality, and blocked opportunities for societal advancement (Cloward & Ohlin, 1960; Gottfredson & Hirschi, 1990; Miller, 1958; Sellin, 1938; Shaw & McKay, 1942).

Each of these avenues is worth exploring and has been explored using methodologically sound techniques in the past. However, what we are suggesting is that researchers not only consider looking at these traditional sociological explanations of delinquency, but also consider the transmission of the values portrayed in the media of the role models of the youth at greatest risk. In our view, the transmission of values serves as a connector to these other explanations. Thus, the purpose of this chapter is not to state that one race is more responsible for crime than any other, but rather to encourage academicians and others to begin looking at some other factors such as the cultural transmission in this crime causation nexus. This clearly will not be an easy task, but one that could pay off ten fold in this connecter is found.

Conclusion and Policy Implications

Juvenile crime and violence is one of the most troubling crimes that we face. When a life is stopped short or a youth's transition to adulthood is put on hold to stand trial for a crime committed, not only does the youth stand to lose, but so does society because it is likely that that child will never reach his full potential.

In the past we have collected and analyzed trends among our nation's youths in terms of the crimes committed and the qualitative aspects of these criminal events. However, we are reaching a point where theory on this aspect of crime and delinquency is at a stand still. Traditional sociological explanations tend to explain these types of crime in the aggregate and more recent studies tend to explain recent fluctuation in these overall rates. However, from our standpoint it is time to extend our knowledge of these types of crimes and include in our theoretical understanding of these crimes the role that the media plays in transmitting a value set that is oftentimes inconsistent with the majority of society. If Simon Lee is correct and the media are not just reporters of the news but rather players in setting the normative structure of society, then it is time we pay attention to how they portray the lifestyles of habits of those who are looked up to. Why is it when an NFL quarterback finances dog fighting, it is news for weeks? However when another athlete admired by all breaks the all-time hit record of Lou Gehrig, it is played on *SportsCenter* for a day and then the story loses its luster. Why is it that an athlete like Derek Jeter does not have his life story told in primetime but others who violate all of our social norms do? Why is it that the media and others do not talk about the good things and charities set up by athletes such as David Robinson and Michael Jordan and others seems to get lost on the back pages of our papers, and stories about Chris Brown, Tupac Shakur, Ray Lewis and others live on in infamy on shows, such as *ET* and *TMZ*, and the blogosphere?

Just what does this mean and how are these stories affecting our nation's youths? These are all issues that need to be explored within the context of how these stories and their portrayal affect the psyche of our nation's youths, specifically the population of youths at greatest risk. The reinstatement of Michael Vick with the Philadelphia Eagles is a testament to the forgiving nature of American society. The press conferences held where he stated he made mistakes in his youth were a great step. But this cannot end here. If Michael Vick wants to truly make a difference, he and other athletes/celebrities who have high-profile encounters with the law need to continue to talk about their problems and how they have are still struggling to overcome them. After all, this is good therapy not just for them, but for the millions of people and youths that follow and idolize them.

While it is too early to tell if the cultural transmission hypothesis will withstand empirical testing, it is clear that community and political leaders should be doing all they can to protect youths. We can no longer afford to turn a blind eye to these violent youths and perpetuate the era of "hip-hop homicide."

Discussion Questions

1. To what extent do you think that juveniles are influenced by the media, sports figures, and the cultural icons of the time?
   a. Is it the media that has created this effect or is it the culture of society that is being transmitted through the media?
2. How has the social context of violence in the media affected the criminality of youth?
3. If youth crime, especially violent youth crime, continues to escalate over the coming years, what does this say about the current practice of having a two part justice system—one for juveniles and another for adults?
4. What is needed to improve the system of justice for violent juveniles?

5. Is it possible to believe that the system of juvenile justice in this country can continue to operate as it has for the past 100 years?

References

Adams, K., Hazlett, R., Ronnau, J., and Surette, R. (2007). Prelimary obervations based upon trend analysis of serious and violent juvenile cases in Orange and Osceola Counties, Florida January 1995 thru December 2006. Orlando, FL: University of Central Florida.

Bailey, W. C., Martin, J. D., and Gray, L. N. (1974). Crime and deterrence: A correlation analysis. *Journal of Research in Crime and Deliquency* 11(2): 124–143.

Bentham, J. (1830). *The rationale of punishment.* London: R. Heward.

Blumstein, A. J. (1995). Youth violence, guns, and the illict-drug indutsry. *The Journal of Criminal Law and Criminology* 86(1), 10–36.

Boy shoots brother dead in video game row. (2009). *Sky News.* http://news.sky.com/skynews/Home/World-News/Mississippi-Boy-9-Shot-Dead-In-Video-Game-Row-In-Marshall-County/Article/200906215300047?f=rss (accessed August 3, 2009).

Caniglia, J. (2009). Wellington teen Daniel Petric gets 23 years for killing mom, shooting dad. *Cleveland Plain Dealer.* http://www.cleveland.com/news/plaindealer/index.ssf?/base/news/1245227634164350.xml&coll=2.

Centers for Disease Control. (2007). *Youth risk behavioral surveillance—United States 2007.*

Centers for Disease Control. (2009). *Youth violence: Facts at a glance.* http://www.cdc.gov/ViolencePrevention/pdf/YV-DataSheet-a.pdf (accessed August 3, 2009).

Cloward, R., and Ohlin, L. (1960). *Delinquency and opportunity.* New York: Free Press.

Davis, G., and Stevenson, H. (2006). Racial socialization experiences and symptoms of depression among black youth. *Journal of Child and Family Studies* 15(3), 293–307.

Dillon, N., and Hutchinson, B. (2009). Chris Brown's sentence for beating up Rihanna delayed by judge. *New York Daily News,* August 5. http://www.nydailynews.com/gossip/2009/08/05/2009-08-05_judge_delays_sentence_for_chris_brown.html.

Federal Bureau of Investigation. (2008). *Supplementary homicide reports for the years 1980–2006.* Washington, DC: U.S. Department of Justice.

Gottfredson, M., and Hirschi, T. (1990). *A general theory of crime.* Stanford, CA: Stanford University Press.

http://bjs.ojp.usdoj.gov/index.cfm?ty=kft&tid=9

Kratcoski, P., Dunn, L., and Kratcoski, D. (1990). *Juvenile delinquency* (3rd ed.). Englewood Cliffs, NJ: Prentice Hall.

Livingstone, S. (1996). On the continuing problem of media effects. In *Mass media and society,* ed. J. Curran and M. Gurevitch, 305–324. London: Arnold.

Miller, W. (1958). Lower class culture as a generating milieu of gang delinquency. *Journal of Social Sciences,* 14: 9–10.

Office of Juvenile Justice and Delinquency Prevention. (2006). *Juvenile offenders and victims: 2006 national report.* Washington, DC: U.S. Department of Justice.

Office of Juvenile Justice and Delinquency Prevention. (2008a). Statistical briefing book. http://ojjdp.ncjrs.gov/ojstatbb/population/qa01401.asp?qaDate=2007 (accessed September 12, 2009).

Office of Juvenile Justice and Delinquency Prevention. (2008b). *Statistical briefing book*, October 24. http://ojjdp.ncjrs.org/ojstatbb/crime/JAR_Display.asp?ID=qa05265 (accessed August 3, 2009).

Peay, J. (1998). The power of the popular. In *Emerging themes in criminology*, ed. T. Newburn and J. Vagg. Loughborough: British Society of Criminology.

Police to ask prosecutors for warrent to arrest Iverson. (2002). *SI.com.* http://sportsillus-trated.cnn.com/basketball/news/2002/07/09/iverson_arrest_ap/.

Radzinowicz, L. (1956). *A history of English criminal law*, Vol. 2/3. London: Stevens.

Schramm, W. (1961). *Television in the lives of our children*. Stanford, CA: Stanford University Press.

Sellin, T. (1938). *Culture, conflict and crime*. New York: Social Science Research Council.

Shaw, C., and McKay, H. (1942). *Juvenile delinquency in urban areas*. Chicago: University of Chicago Press.

Sheridan, C. (2000). *NBA's Iverson to change offensive rap lyrics*. ESPN Sports. http://abc-news.go.com/Sports/Story?id=100294&page=1.

Snyder, H., and Sickmund, M. (2006). *Juvenile offenders and victims: 2006 national report*. Washington, DC: National Center for Juvenile Justice and Deliquency Prevention.

Wilson, J. Q. (1975). *Thinking about crime*. New York: Basic Books.

Zimring, F. E. (2004). The Discrete character of high-lethality youth violence. *Annals of the New York Academy of Science* 1036: 290–299.

Index